Separating

The Astrology of Break-ups, Divorce, and Other Partings

Armand Diaz, Ph.D.

Integral Transformation

Published by Integral Transformation in the United States of America and the United Kingdom.

© 2014 Integral Transformation, LLC

Cover design and © illustration by Loretta Lopez

First Edition: March, 2014

ISBN: 978-0-9894163-1-3

Acknowledgements

I'm a member of a fortunate generation of astrologers. We get to stand on the shoulders of all of those who came before us and we can learn from all of those who are still with us. Never before in history has access across time and place been so open and easy. I have learned astrology from many, many people, from the past and present. I would therefore like to thank the astrological community, past and present.

Special thanks go to John Marchesella. I learned astrology in a very short time thanks to John, who imparted astrological wisdom in a way that seemed to me like Plato's anamnesis, a kind of *unforgetting*.

My colleagues in the universe of transpersonal astrology also deserve my ongoing thanks. Eric Meyers, Andrew Smith, Faye Cossar, Chet Zdrowski, and Rafael Nasser have provided me with the intellectual dialogue and emotional support for the past several years, and have done much to shape my views of astrology. Anne Whitaker and Ed Snow have been ongoing sources of support for my work.

Maria DeSimone, Natalie Delahaye, and Margaret Grey graciously agreed to read the book and provide their comments. In this time when we all feel pressured and pulled in a thousand directions, I know it was a huge favor to ask, and I am truly grateful.

This book began as a presentation, and has evolved through many formats over the years. I've had an opportunity to present this material to the astrological community and receive the response of my fellow astrologers. Thanks to Bonnie Simms, Lenore Grafmuller, Mark James, Linda Furiate, Linda Byrd, Nora Jean Stone, Kari Noren-Hoshal, Julene Packer-Louis, Ena Stanley, Donna Van Toen, Heather Horton, Ian Waisler, Linea Van Horn,

Donna Woodwell, and many others who helped to make that possible.

The board of NCGR-New York City helps make astrology fun while providing excellent educational and professional programs. There's nothing quite like eating cookies and celery on Friday evenings while listening to the insights of some of the finest astrologers I know.

When I asked Loretta Lopez to design the book cover, I knew I would be happy with the results, but I didn't expect to find myself torn between so many brilliant options. I think I have the covers for my next three books already selected!

I would also like to thank my clients. My Scorpio ascendant attracts people at serious turning points in their lives, and I have had the opportunity to learn a great deal as my clients have traversed some challenging territory. I was not taking notes, but this book will show that I took many learning experiences to heart.

Contents

There's more on relationships and other aspects of astrology at IntegralAstrology.net!

Preface

Astrologers spend a good deal of time in the seventh house, the house of relationship. While we work with many other areas of life—in fact the entire range of human (and some nonhuman) experience comes under the gaze of astrologers—relationship captures much of our attention. People want to know when they will meet someone with whom they can connect, they want to know the potential of a new partnership, and, not infrequently, they want to understand the stresses that are within the relationship. And people also come to astrologers when they are contemplating, fearing, experiencing, or recovering from a break-up, separation, or divorce.

Relationships are an area where people often invest a great deal of their emotional currency, and where they are often reticent to withdraw their funds even when the investment is clearly not paying off. There are a lot of reasons for that, and we'll explore them as we go along. For now, we only need to recognize that partnerships tend to be such a significant area in our lives that they can gain a kind of power over us. We say that *we have relationships*, but in many cases *our relationships have us*. Leaving a relationship or having a partner leave can be a traumatic event in a person's life.

We meet many other souls as we move through life, and in one way or another they teach us about love and who we really are at a fundamental level. We connect deeply with some of these souls—as lovers but also as friends, family, and in other ways— and we find great joy in these connections. Alas, we are on this plane to learn and evolve, not to bask in the joy of love. Or perhaps we *are* here to bask in the joy of love, but most of us have quite a bit of learning to do before we can really live that way. Despite our deep connections, despite the love we feel, our complex lives often don't mesh with the transcendent soul connections.

This book is about the ending of relationships. My intention is to help astrologers to help their clients by understanding the dynamics of break-ups, separations, and divorce from an astrological perspective. It isn't about predicting the end of a partnership, but about deepening awareness of what is taking place when two people go their separate ways after weeks, months, years, or decades together.

The premise that we will explore is that while relationship endings can be difficult, they also contain the promise of greater personal awareness and growth. Difficult times are frequently powerful catalysts for our souls' evolution and there is often rich meaning to be discovered in the end of a relationship. Even on a more basic emotional level, the end of a relationship need not be viewed as something to be feared—in fact our clients are as likely to leave a relationship as to have their partners leave.

While understanding that break-ups can be difficult, we won't be assuming that a separation is necessarily painful. And even if it is, most people will emerge from the challenging period stronger, more aware, and hopefully capable of greater and more satisfying love.

Introduction

It's About Us...

I don't think my grandparents had a relationship.

They were married for more than 60 years, had three children and six grandchildren, and they loved and aggravated each other, just like people in relationships do. They had roles and responsibilities. They certainly related to each other. But I'm still not entirely sure they had a relationship in the way that we think about it today. That is, I don't know if they had a concept of themselves as existing within a partnership, an awareness of *the relationship* as a kind of third entity that existed along side of both of them. Another way to say it is that I don't know that they really reflected on the way that related to each other, with subsequent ongoing assessment and adjustment.

It's different today. We certainly *do* have relationships, and we think about them a lot. Some of us even spend more energy thinking about the character and quality of our relationships than we do actually paying attention to our partners. We have all kinds of ideas about what a good relationship would and should be like. We read books that tell us how to work on our relationships, and we describe relationships as healthy or unhealthy, as though they were living beings—which in a sense they are. We frequently reflect on the status of our partnerships, and many of us give them top priority in our lives.

Things have changed a lot in the past few decades. Yes, we now focus on and think about relationship in a more abstract and reflective way. But the structure of relationship itself has also changed significantly since the 1960s. We'll go through a brief astro-history of partnership in a later chapter, but it's easy to see that within a short period of time many of the assumptions people had about relating were upended. Astrologers often point out that during the Neptune in Scorpio years (1957-1971) the development of the birth control pill (Neptune: drugs; Scorpio: sex) liberated people from the fear that sex would result in pregnancy, and so opened up the possibility of short-term intimate relationships (shorter than marriage for life, at least). But it was the passage of Uranus and Pluto through the sign of relationship, Libra, from 1968 through 1984 that really got us thinking about relationship as a thing as such.

If you remember the 1970s, you'll recall that the self-help movement really began during the decade, and a great deal of the focus was on relationships. The Women's Movement was another factor that changed the status quo in the area of relationship, and the transition of many women into the workforce had powerful repercussions on partnerships. A combination of social and economic forces, together with a general boost in the level of self-awareness brought about by the turbulent yet creative 1960s all led to the establishment of the relationship as an entity. The liberalization of divorce laws throughout the Western world was both a result of and a catalyst for changes, and an important one. As more people began openly living together without marriage and divorce became a more accessible option, and with sex (temporarily) more open and free of long-term commitment, it was much easier to think about relationship apart from marriage. Thus, we transitioned from strict, Saturnian, structured, legally based marriage as the primary vehicle for partnership to the more flexible, Uranian, open, feeling based *relationship*.

There are many advantages to having relationships exist as separate entities. We truly do see the relationship as a third party:

10

there's you, there's me, and then there's *us*. With the addition of this third entity, we can separate the individuals from the patterns of relationship that they create. I don't need to blame you or make you change – at least not directly. Rather, I can point out that something in our relationship is a bit out of balance. I don't need to blame you if I am no longer enjoying your company: it is easier and kinder to say that the relationship no longer seems to be going anywhere. And it's not just a matter of semantics, because we can genuinely respect that where we are each going as individuals may or may not work for the relationship. It truly helps to be able to ask for changes in the relationship without actually demanding that your partner change who they are, although such change may well be implied. The relationship is also a shared project, something that can be *worked on* (although it would be nicer if it were *played with*) by both people in a joint effort, and in that sense it helps to keep us interested and responsible.

Describing relationships as a thing or an entity is actually a little misleading, because it implies a static object. To say that we work on a relationship is like saying that we work on a car. A car stays more or less the same, except for the occasional tune up or oil change, and perhaps sometimes a major repair, but it generally keeps the same form. A relationship is more like an activity, such as driving, where continual adjustments are necessary, even on straight roads. In fact, rather than thinking about them as objects, I think it is best to view a relationship as a *process*. In many disciplines today, we are beginning to move away from the view of static things towards an appreciation of processes. Physicists have demonstrated that the universe is really quite dynamic and even apparently solid objects are in constant motion at the subatomic level, so it is appropriate that we understand that relationships and the individuals that participate in them are also processes and not objects. You, me, and us are all in a state of flux, developing, evolving, and morphing into new forms. Just as thinking about relationship itself is freeing, so thinking about relationship as process helps us to understand the dynamics of relationship changes, including break-ups. With a process

11

approach to relationship, we can begin to see why relationships end without needing to place blame on anyone, or even see the parting as a necessarily bad thing.

That's important, because in addition to the emotional pain of separation due to the loss of the partner, there are also often feelings of shame, guilt, or failure. Not too many years ago, people in their late teens would legally and socially promise to be with each other until death parted them. Today, more than half of marriages in the United States end in divorce, many people who marry do so much later in life, and many others decide not to marry at all. Despite these profound changes to the social landscape of partnership, many people feel that they have failed when a relationship ends. Our images and expectations have apparently not changed as much our behavior. In many ways, the outer planets seem to be trying to jar us loose from our preconceived ideas about intimacy, but many of us aren't going willingly.

When we switch to a process approach to relationships, we can see that individuals need to grow in new directions, and relationships also need to transform themselves. Ending is part of the process. Sooner or later, we all depart from all of our relationships. If people are moving in different directions, or the relationship no longer has the cohesion to continue, we don't need to look at it as a failure or analyze what went wrong. We can also see that a person's relationship process may develop over multiple relationships, and if we take a really long view of things, we can at least hypothesize that it evolves over many lifetimes. That this particular relationship is coming to an end begins to look less traumatic—at least from the astrologer's perspective— when we take a more evolutionary process view.

We may also consider that the ability to have shorter relationships contributes to speeding up the process of evolution, as we can learn from multiple partners in a single lifetime. Of course, you could also argue that a lifetime relationship helps a person to go deeper into relationship dynamics than a series of shorter partnerships. Perhaps we need to learn different kinds of lessons at different points in our individual and collective histories. The important point is that we can remove negative judgments about the ending of relationships if we understand them as learning processes and growth opportunities.

It's Not So Bad

I don't want to minimize the pain that can be experienced in the loss of a relationship. Almost all of us can recall the grief and uncertainty that surrounded the end of one of our partnerships, and some of us look back with regret decades later. It is a big deal.

On the other hand, we should never prejudge the effect that the ending of a relationship will have on a person. It could be tragic, but it could also be liberating. In almost any case, it will be an important growth experience that has potential to help the person become more open and freer. It isn't an easy process, but we need to get away from the idea that it is necessarily *bad*. And what may be viewed as traumatic at one point in time can be celebrated later on in life. Plenty of people feel that a divorce is essentially the end of their lives, while in retrospect it is viewed as the real beginning.

As with any kind of change, it isn't unusual for there to be some fear associated with the ending of a partnership, but fear isn't an indication of the ultimate value of any experience. Needless to say, some people have an easier time than others with this particular kind of change, something we'll discuss in the chapter on the modes. For now, we need to acknowledge that some people aren't all that upset by the ending of even very long-term relationships, and the consulting astrologer shouldn't assume that the person is feeling bad. Many times, they are looking for encouragement to make a move.

It's worth remembering that our clients may be the breaker or the broken-with when a relationship ends. The astrology is not necessarily going to be clear on that, although there are indications of whether the person was feeling the need for change. It's especially important not to judge the ending of a relationship negatively when someone is contemplating leaving, as it can take the energy away from someone who really wants to make a change. It's probably best to explore feelings around the ending of the relationship, to help the client assess what they would miss as well as what they would be happy to leave behind.

Above all, we don't want to be like a physician who will use all possible means to save the patient. The assumption that the ending of a relationship is a bad thing is highly problematic to begin with, and it is certainly the case that not all relationships need to be saved. We want to empower our clients to make their own decisions and help them realize their full potential in any situation. We can hand them a box of tissues and be sympathetic to the grief *they* are feeling, but we don't need to contribute to it by reinforcing the idea that something terrible has happened. We don't want to be insensitive, either, but it is all too easy to play to assumptions that aren't necessarily valid for our clients.

What This Book *Isn't*

Years ago, I was taking a course in astrology where we'd all bring in people to have their chart done. The students in the class, with the help of the teacher, would assess the chart and its transits for a while, before the volunteer would start to offer some information.

One week, a young woman came in. She was married, very pretty, and seemed a bit shy, although the situation didn't help many people's social comfort level. All I remember about her astrologically is that she was about a year shy of her Saturn return and her ascendant was in the early degrees of Gemini. It was the mid to late 1990s, and Pluto had just entered her 7th house of partnership. The class did the sort of nervous, giggling, eye rolling speculation that astrology students love to do. We skirted around things a great deal, but it was clear that some dire prediction about her relationship had to be made. A couple of the men in the class became very supportive and caring, as though they thought she might soon be single.

After a while, the teacher asked the woman what was happening in her relationship, assessing the situation by simply stating that it seemed like something big might be going on. And indeed it was—she was pregnant. Her relationship was in the process of deep, transformative change, just as the astrology had suggested, but it wasn't in a state of irreparable crisis, as the students were so ready to believe.

My point is even considering all the available astrological information—house rulerships, dignities, and so on—we still don't know how things will play out. We can't know how an astrological transit will manifest because we don't know the person behind the chart. We don't know how they've handled transits in the past, and we don't know how much consciousness they are bringing to the their natal chart. We don't know how social, cultural, religious, family, and personal values and beliefs will affect their decisions. And astrological transits don't manifest in just one way, although astrologers often look for the boldest and most obvious manifestation. Rather, they play out all over the landscape of a person's life, affecting many areas in different ways. That's why this book is not about predicting the end of relationships.

Of course, if you do know the person, if they are a friend or a regular client, you might be able to take a reasonable guess. Sure, someone whose relationship has been under a strain for years may indeed break it off when Uranus conjuncts his or her Venus. But don't make predictions anyway. Pluto to Venus may mean the end of the relationship, but it could also mean going to therapy, going through a deep process together, and renewing the partnership. It may not seem likely with a particular couple, but leave open the possibility. You don't need to tell anyone what is going to happen to them. The assumption in this book is that the person is already in the midst of a break-up, and they are aware of it.

This book is also not a repair manual for relationships. Granted, with this area of life, "it's not over 'til it's over," and even then it may not be over, so we will be looking at common strategies people use to repair their partnerships, and the healthy and unhealthy consequences that may ensue. It could be that the couple gets back together, of course, but in this book we aren't working with the assumption that that is the case—we're assuming it is unlikely.

What This Book *Is*

This book is a guide to understanding the different styles of break-ups, based primarily on the transits of the four outer planets. It is also a guide to how different styles of relating will affect the perception and experience of a separation, because someone who is more likely to accept change may have a very different perception than one who is more stability-oriented. In other words, Uranus transits feel different to an Aries than they do to a Taurus.

Knowledge of outer planet transits in a break-up is useful for understanding the dynamics of a separation, but it is also the key to recognizing the challenges that are faced and the opportunities that are present. The assumption is that any and all break-ups involve the potential for greater personal awareness and spiritual growth—after all, everything does! Specifics offer clues as to how to engage the growth opportunities, and we can share these with our clients to help guide them through the process. Yet as astrologers we also need to be open to learning, and we need to recognize that we too are in a continual process of growth and evolving understanding. This book isn't a comprehensive list of all the possibilities, it is an outline that can be filled in in an infinite number of ways.

So, we know that this book isn't about predicting break-ups, but about understanding them. We know that we as astrologers shouldn't judge the ultimate value of a separation, but we can help our clients to understand the process and meaning of the process. Now, let's start looking at relationships...

Chapter 1
The Moon

When you think of the astrology of relationships, it might be that the moon doesn't pop into your mind right away. But the moon is a crucial part of the relationship picture because it is so closely tied into our most basic needs for security and nurturance. It's no secret that in our adult relationships we tend to look for, recreate, and try to resolve our early relationships with our parents, but we don't need to look back that far in order to get an understanding of how the moon affects our partnerships.

The moon represents how we seek comfort and security, and this will naturally affect our choice of partners. That is, to an extent we are looking for the moon in our partner, trying to get the other person to provide what we need to feel secure and safe in the world. That's a big job for another person, especially since that person also has his or her own security needs. We often try to strike a bargain with our partners, asking them to be our comfort zone, and in exchange we will be theirs'. The problem is, frequently, that our partners aren't thrilled about being our personal safety zone. Truth be told, when you are the container for another person's insecurities and fears, it can be rather tiring, especially as they continue to find more things for you to carry. The only time it works out successfully is when one partner tacitly agrees to be the others' mother or father, offering one-sided care and support, and that isn't necessarily going to be the most growth-oriented relationship imaginable.

During a break-up, the moon also represents how a person will try to find support and solace. If you think the moon isn't too important as a relationship planet, take a look and see how people act when they are in the process of splitting from a long-term partnership: they often appear to be the very incarnation of their moon. One of the terms used to describe the difficulty children have being parted from the parent is *separation anxiety*, and break-ups will often trigger almost child-like anxiety, as they are, after all, *separations*.

There are a number of factors about the moon that are worth noting in relationship to a break-up. These include the sign and house placement, and significant aspects to the moon. Use the following as a general guide, but you'll find that much of what you know about the moon applies to break-ups, and relationships in general. It is simply more intensified and obvious during the process of separation. In the list below, I have included both sign and house placement. The sign is more primary and usually more obvious, but you can look to the house for a secondary layer of understanding. Expect that the house placement will show up in more concrete ways than the sign, while the sign will usually be a better description of the person's internal state. However, because the house placement is also likely to be less prominent, the behaviors associated with it may not grab your attention.

Moon in Aries/First House – In a relationship: the person looks for the other to provide a degree of excitement and energy. They expect the other person to keep it lively and feel most comfortable when the relationship is active and dynamic. In a break-up: the person with moon in Aries will want to know that they can take care of his or her self, that they can be self-reliant in all areas of life. Getting things going again, starting over, moving on, and getting back on track are priorities, and the danger is a rebound relationship.

Moon in Taurus/Second House – In a relationship: the person looks for the other to support (not necessarily fulfill) basic security needs, to be reliable in sensual, financial, and other aspects of the material plane. The partner doesn't have to take the lead in these areas, but they are expected to be present and participate. In a break-up: the person with moon in Taurus will often retreat into their material possessions, perhaps treating himself to a luxury item or otherwise proving to herself that the world is still a safe place because goodies can be had.

Moon in Gemini/Third House – In a relationship: although this moon is probably best known as having a light, chatty style, I have found that there is a slight tendency towards a kind of depression in Gemini moons. It almost seems as though the person is looking for their lost twin, and seeks to find it in the partner. There is a malleable quality to the Gemini moon that can be comfortable as long as the partner seems content. In a break-up: there is a tendency to try to establish a new routine as quickly as possible. With the partner gone, the space may be filled with friends, relatives, and others who happen to be nearby. If there is a tendency to go back to past, pre-partnership routines, this could have an awkward and stifling effect.

Moon in Cancer/Fourth House – In a relationship: security needs are paramount, and the person wants to know the partner will always be there. These security needs can create problems ranging from jealousy to fear of even small amounts of change. In a break-up: the person will wish to establish a new home base as quickly as possible. They may be very focused on their physical living space, finances, and other material signs of security, but they may also retreat back towards their family, hometown, and the values with which they grew up. At an extreme, the growth and development they experienced in breaking away from home can be seen as mistaken folly, and they may become *true believers* in the values of their family, culture, and religion.

Moon in Leo/Fifth House – In a relationship: there is a need to feel and be treated specially. Extra attention and support are important for a person with a Leo moon, and they naturally look to the partner as at least one source of these. In a break-up: the person with a Leo moon will often look to others to reassure them that they are special. Leo moons want to be wanted, and at times there can be a need to prove that they can still be attractive to others. Areas of life that don't have to do with relationship, but in which the person shines or excels, can become the focus during a break-up.

Moon in Virgo/Sixth House – In a relationship: there is a tendency to be helpful, but in a dutiful, non-clingy type of way. In a more pronounced way than the moon in Gemini, Virgo moons can display a Mercurial on-off attitude in their affections. Often there is not a great show of emotion coming from people with a Virgo moon, although of course they feel as deeply as anyone else. In a break-up: Virgo is a self-contained sign, and maintaining that self-containment is important when stresses occur. There is a tendency to *soldier on* with life, sometimes not giving adequate attention to their own feelings.

Moon in Libra/Seventh House – In a relationship: maintaining harmony is a priority. Ideally, for the person with the moon in the sign of the scales, the relationship itself is harmonious, but at the very least it should appear to be so when presented to the public. In a break-up: Moon in Libra will want to know that everything is okay and that emotional equilibrium can and will be restored. There is a mild tendency to go back to more traditional ways of relating. For example, if a couple was living together before the break-up, the person with moon in Libra may begin to think that marriage is a better form for long-term partnerships. It may be hard for moon in Libra to express feelings to others.

Moon in Scorpio/Eighth House – In a relationship: there may be a vulnerability that is not easily expressed as such. In fact, it may be that the person with the moon in Scorpio presents as a power player who will not take any guff from their partner. In a break-up: there are a number of ways that separations can manifest for the person with the moon in this sign, and it has perhaps the most positive and negative potentials. It is the ability to let go, and to recognize the need for the relationship to end that is the pivot point. If there is a recognition that the relationship was over, then a period of appropriate grief is followed by a rebirth and healthy readiness for the next stage of relationship. If there is a holding on to the partnership, then emotional power struggles—between the partners or within the partner with a Scorpio moon—can lead to ongoing conflict and chronic scab-picking.

Moon in Sagittarius/Ninth House – In a relationship: the person looks for the partner to be fun, to aid in exploration and in keeping life lively. In a break-up: the person with a moon in the sign of the archer will want to know that life—as they want to live it—will go on. They may emphasize philosophical approaches to life, some exploring new spiritual avenues while others retreat to more deeply entrenched in traditional beliefs, such as religious or political dogma. Sagittarius is an expansive and flexible sign when it is searching for the truth, but it can be rather rigid when it thinks it's found it. The stress of a break-up can push some Sagittarian moons back to old-time religion.

Moon in Capricorn/Tenth House – In a relationship: there can be a tendency to shoulder responsibility and make sure things get done. Capricorn moons are responsible, and they often take care of a lot of the work that needs to be done, including planning major projects and managing routine tasks. In a breakup: this moon is one of those that will put out a lot of effort to be sure that they can take care of themselves. If a relationship is ending, the person may throw themselves into career, housework, and other forms of work. It can be as though they need to convince themselves that they will still be productive.

Moon in Aquarius/Eleventh House – In a relationship: it's not true that Aquarian moons are cold, but like their Libran cousins they

21

want things to be a certain way and can be demanding about it. Principles, rather than appearance, are what motivate Aquarius, although the specifics vary from person to person. In a break-up: Aquarian moons can be focused on being treated fairly and each party doing what they consider to be right. There can be a tendency to have a chilly, analytical approach that guards deeper feelings, and a focus on the reasons why the partnership didn't last.

Moon in Pisces/Twelfth House – In a relationship: Pisces moons are deeply sensitive and empathic, and there can be a tendency to blend the other's feelings with their own. The great strength is of course empathy, but the danger is identifying with the partner's feelings and a blurring of emotional boundaries. In a break-up: escapism comes in many forms, and a Pisces moon may avail itself of one form or another. An ability to dissociate can be a useful strategy for Pisces moons, but what it really needs is to know is that it is still connected to something or someone in some way.

The Moon in Hard Aspect to the Outer Planets

The moon represents security needs, and these tend to be threatened during the loss of a relationship. Because the outer planets tend to describe the quality of a break-up, it is very helpful to know if there is any relationship between the outer planets and the moon in the natal chart. Although such a natal chart relationship may not describe the quality of the separation, it is very likely to color the person's perception of the process. Much has already been written by astrologers about the moon in aspect to other planets, but we'll focus here on how security issues can emerge during a break-up.

Moon and Saturn

When the moon is in a conjunction, square, or opposition to Saturn, there may be a slight tendency to emotional depression.

This doesn't indicate any kind of clinical depression, of course, but simply a kind of sadness, a tendency to look on the dark side of things. The person may have the tacit assumption that his or her emotional needs will never be met, or will not be regarded as important by others. On the other hand, Moon/Saturn contacts can mean a great deal of self-sufficiency, and can indicate the ability to avoid wallowing in difficulty emotional places.

During a break-up, Moon/Saturn people may express an accepting, almost dulled response to the loss, although they may feel it very intensely. The importance of showing themselves that they are physically, financially, and otherwise okay is often very prominent. "Yes, it is sad," they seem to say, "but I will get through this."

Moon and Uranus

The moon in a hard aspect to Uranus often indicates a very changeable emotional picture. Ups and downs follow on each other quickly, and they may be felt very intensely. At the core of Moon/Uranus aspects is a need for emotional independence, and at some point the person needs to feel that they are emotionally free from constricting circumstances and anything that would limit their feelings.

When a break-up occurs, it is important for the person to assess how they are feeling about the transition occurring in their life. Possibly, they are feeling excited about the possibility of moving on with their lives, yet it could also be that they are feeling that yet another relationship has exploded and that they will never have romantic happiness. Part of the response may be related to the moon sign: moon in Cancer may feel anxious about the Uranian lack of stability, while moon in Aries may be energized by it.

Moon and Neptune

The moon is sensitized by any contact with Neptune, and people with these aspects typically feel things very deeply. There is often a connection to the spiritual world that goes through the emotions, an empathy that can open up to real compassion, but one that can also be overwhelming to the ego.

In fact, the empathic nature of Moon/Neptune may mean that during a break-up they *feel beyond their own feelings*, so that they resonate with a deeper consciousness of suffering. It is also possible that they may empathize with the sense of loss their partner is feeling, and that can be a problem if the Moon/Neptune person is the one initiating the break-up. It isn't true, however, that Moon/Neptune people will fare any better or worse than anyone else during a separation. They may indeed have more dramatic experiences, but the astrologer should not expect that the end result will be either enlightenment or complete dissolution of the ego (for better or worse).

Moon and Pluto

The many manifestations of Pluto contacts with the moon in the natal chart are well known. Many astrologers will immediately jump to conclusions about a controlling mother undermining the individual's sense of independence, and that does sometimes occur. What is most likely, however, is that there is a history of some deep emotional experiences that continue to influence the person in subtle ways. There may be an early loss, or some traumatic event, or perhaps just the perception of trauma. Maybe the effects of a past life are being felt. What is very typical, however, is that there is a kind of dread attached to deep emotional experiences, and the person both approaches *and* avoids them. In terms of relationship, Moon/Pluto people both crave and fear intimacy—even more than the rest of us.

During a break-up, the question may seem to be whether the person feels that they are a victim or the aggressor, and both possibilities exist whether the Moon/Pluto person or their partner initiates the break-up. In fact, it is not unlikely that the person will begin feeling that he or she is the victim, and this rouses them to act like an aggressor, trying to take control of the situation (and that *may* be a healthy response). However, the victim/aggressor dichotomy may not be present, and may be false if it is present. More basic is that security needs tend to run very strong with Moon/Pluto people, and they may feel that the best defense is a good offense.

Summary

The last thing we want to do is to pigeonhole people according to their astrology, and since there are only twelve signs and more than seven billion people on the planet, there has to be a great deal of variation in how any one astrological factor expresses itself. Aspect to the moon, house position, and the signs that the other planets are in will all have a significant effect—along with culture, education, and personal history. Don't tell your clients what they feel! It's much more helpful to use information about the moon to guide your questions and help to frame the emotions that clients express.

Chapter Two
The Sun

At heart, the sun is about our deepest, truest self. The sun in an astrological chart describes the soul's purpose in this incarnation. The light that energizes everything else in the chart is colored by sun's sign, and the area of life where it will manifest most clearly is found by the house position.

In practice, the sun is often thought of on a somewhat less profound level. On a lower level, we tend to associate the sun with the things in our lives that point to our deeper purpose. In other words, the sun represents *what we identify with in our lives*, those things that seem to at least indicate where we should be and who we really are. I often tell my students that the sun is what you tell others about yourself when you first meet. If you are introduced to someone at a party, you might say that you are an accountant, that you're married and have three children, for example. Those are the things about your life with which you identify, which seem to you to describe who you are. They are *approximations* to your sun, although they may or may not be good representations of your actual soul purpose. Sometimes we can only scrape together a very vague sense of who we really are from the material in our lives.

26

In old-time astrology, the sun and moon figured very prominently in relationship analysis. Basically, the moon was thought to represent the emotional, feeling nature, and was associated with women. The sun was the outgoing, active principle and was associated with men. Today, we might hesitate to say that the sun is masculine and the moon feminine, avoiding assignment of physical gender to the planets, but back in the day gender roles were very tightly prescribed. With the direct association of sun with men and the moon with women, a harmonious relationship between these planets was seen as key. Basically, the woman's moon in a relationship was going to be the feminine side of the man, and the man's sun was going to be the masculine side of the woman. That is, the man and woman were going to farm out their feminine and masculine sides to the other person. Simply put, the man in a relationship was going to act as the solar principle for the woman, and the woman was going to act as the lunar principle for the man.

Most of us today bristle against such limited gender-based stereotypes, although a few traditional folks might still resonate with this kind of thinking. It was evident in many places through the 1960s, and I can remember being a child and hearing women introduce themselves by their husband's name, as in, "Hello, I'm Mrs. Darren Stevens." It was a way of saying, "My husband is my identity," or astrologically, "My husband is my sun." Women have come a long way in recent decades and are unlikely to farm out their solar functions to male partners. Men have had a slightly more difficult time in owning their emotional, lunar sides, in part because modern Western society bends towards outgoing, masculine, yang values. Still, both men and women are much more likely to accept both sides of themselves, and solar and lunar functions are both incorporated into each gender. Of course, not all relationships are between a man and a woman, and the increasing acceptance of different relationship patterns is both a result and a cause of greater psychic wholeness within individuals.

While the moon represents some of the ego-based needs that we try to resolve in our relationships with others, and also shows us where a person is likely to go if they are wounded by changes in a partnership, the sun is much less likely to have such an overt role in break-ups, except that both men and women *do* tend to define themselves and create their self-image (the lower solar function) based in part on their relationships. To the extent that they do that, a break-up represents a change in who they are and how they see themselves: if they have self-defined as someone who is in a particular relationship and that relationship ends, it is a blow to their sense of self.

What you really need to listen for is how much the person has identified themselves—their being—with their relationship, as that is where the sun can really be significant in the process. The work for the client, with a little guidance from the astrologer, is to disentangle the sense of "I" from the "us" of the relationship. For people that have made a very tight identification, that can be as traumatic as losing any other part of the self-system, and we shouldn't underestimate the dangers.

It sounds like (and thankfully largely is) a remnant of 19th century novels to talk about dying from a broken heart, but such things can happen. For example, we can switch gears a bit and look at career, another area people tend to identify with very closely. When the economy took a downturn in the late 1970s and early 1980s, many executives in business lost their jobs. At the time, most executive positions were held by middle-aged men, and an awkwardly large percentage of these unemployed executives had heart attacks.

Now, it's pretty unlikely that a client who goes through even a tough break up will wind up dying of a broken heart, but as the example from the business world shows, it isn't entirely impossible. The sun is both our sense of identity and our physical (and emotional) heart, after all. What we need to be aware of is that someone who has identified with a relationship so totally is likely to feel cut off from their heart—their vitality, courage, enthusiasm, and sense of purpose.

We don't need to consider the individual's sun sign and house placement with the same kind of specificity we did with the moon, but it is helpful to consider some aspects to the sun that can have an effect on relationships and the way they end. The following is a general guide, offering some hints to keep in mind as you work with clients. Remember always that these are just typical patterns and that other chart factors, as well as the degree of awareness the person has about his or her self, will modify or even nullify these generalizations.

Sun conjunct Venus suggests that the person's sense of self and love life are blended. This does not mean that the person is more likely to suffer a sense of identity loss when they are separated, however. People with the sun and Venus conjunct often assume that relationship and love are part of life, and they can have a less clingy, driven need for relationship.

Sun semisquare Venus can be more difficult. With these two planets at the maximum distance from each other, it can seem like relationship and the rest of life are on very different pages. By progression, the meeting of the two celestial bodies is often considered the time when people wake up to a sense of what love means in their lives, and with this aspect the conjunction will not happen until the person is in their mid-forties. Because love can seem somewhat elusive to people with this placement, they may tend to cling to relationships more tightly, afraid that the love they have is all they will ever have.

Sun in hard aspect to Saturn can have difficulty handling break-ups because they tend to judge themselves rather harshly, and can see the end of a relationship as a failure. When the *sun is in easy aspect to Saturn*, transitions are handled more easily because the person has an innate sense of structure that isn't quite so dependent on others. Not infrequently, the person can shift the focus to work, career, and other aspects of life.

29

Sun in hard aspect to Uranus generally leads to a certain amount of flexibility in terms of identification with relationship. These people tend to reinvent themselves often, so they can usually manage change fairly well, at least after a point in life when they get used to dealing with the somewhat erratic influence of Uranus. Those with the *sun in easy aspect to Uranus* make the changes fairly smoothly from an early point in life.

Sun in hard aspect to Neptune is potentially difficult as the sense of identity is inherently porous. It is often very easy to identify with a partner or a relationship, and the same factor that can lead to such wonderful highs at the beginning of a partnership can bring about deep lows at the end. When the *sun is in a soft aspect to Neptune*, things often go better, although it may be that escapism is the strategy of choice for dealing with challenges.

Sun in hard aspect to Pluto can manifest in many ways during a separation. There can be a sense of loss of part of the self, and that can result in a deep struggle. The loss may extend to the person's core and result in a deeply transformative, death-rebirth (but remember death comes first!) experience. But it may also be that although they die a little for it, the person with sun in hard aspect to Pluto doesn't allow the feelings to go very deep and coldly walks away. When the *sun is in easy aspect to Pluto*, a sense of power and continuity of self usually prevails, and major damage to the sense of self is unlikely when a relationship ends.

These are a few possibilities for each scenario, to give you an idea of the patterns associated with each aspect. In some ways, the sun in aspect to the outer planets is a preview of what we'll be covering about relationship and break-up patterns throughout the book, but in this chapter I've restricted the discussion to the sense of self indicated by the sun.

Chapter 3
Mars

I feel that Mars is often the forgotten relationship planet. Astrologers know that the planet associated with drive, assertion, and sexuality is part of the relationship picture, but there isn't very much emphasis placed upon it. That seems to me to be a mistake, although one that is understandable in a historic context. As I've said, relationship—as a thing in itself—is a fairly new phenomenon. In the 1970s, when Uranus and Pluto were passing through Libra, we did a lot of work on this area of life, and we did a lot of thinking about it.

One important insight of the time was the differentiation of love from sex. Although it may not sound like much today, before we really began to think about relationship these two things were often confused and conflated with each other. The blending of desire and drive, on the one hand, with feeling and relatedness, on the other, often led to thinking something along the lines of, "if you desire it, you love it." The result of that could easily be all kinds of aggression and even violence in the name of love.

Differentiating the Venusian feeling function from the Martial drive was a necessary step in our collective evolution of love and relationship. Despite some fine insights into the nature of love in classical times, there wasn't much said on this theme until the 12th century troubadours and their songs of courtly love.

31

Interestingly, a typical facet of their tradition was unobtainable or unrequited love. With the sexual desire thwarted by circumstances (usually a powerful husband standing in the way), the energy of Mars was channeled into the more refined domain of Venus. In other words, out of the frustration of sexual desire emerged a more lofty, conceptualized, vision of romantic love. It's not that the energy of Mars disappeared or was totally transmuted—that would place it out of the range of human love altogether—but rather the active principle of Mars was put in service of the values of Venus.

The next step in this simplified story of romantic love is found in the literature of the 19th century. Stendhal, Flaubert, Goethe, and other Romantic era authors (writing under the spell of newly-discovered Neptune) re-energized the courtly love of the troubadours with tales of the agonies and ecstasies of love that never finds satisfaction (at least not for long). Once again, Mars took a back seat to Venus.

Yet these few outcroppings in the refined artistic realms of Venus and Neptune did not reflect common thinking and values on the subject of love. For most people, the erotic sensibility was an undifferentiated blending of sexuality and feeling. Teasing these two domains apart from each other was tricky work, and that had to wait until a number of changes had occurred. The work began in earnest when Uranus and Pluto were in Libra in the 1970s.

The rewards of separating love and sex (or love and lust) were great. For one thing, it became apparent that just because one was filled with desire for someone did not mean that one really loved that person. People became more finely tuned to the difference, and began to understand that, "I love you" might really mean "I want to have sex with you." Armed with that knowledge, feelings were less likely to be hurt. The differentiation of love and sex also allowed for sex without the weighty commitment of love, if both (or all) parties were clear about it from the start. Thus, we were free to have sex without love, and we could (as always) love without sex.

Having differentiated love and sex, we could now work on either one separately. It was possible to work on our relating in areas apart from sexuality, so that we could open up discussion about our roles within partnership, where the relationship was going, and how we felt about one another. At the same time, we could also discuss sex and desire apart from other areas of relationship. It became possible to recognize that one was sexually (dis)satisfied while being emotionally (un)happy. We were also in the process of becoming more open to sharing our feelings about all of these issues. It was very liberating.

Unfortunately, although perhaps understandably given the Libran emphasis of the 1970s, we followed tradition of the troubadours and the Romantics by putting Mars in service to Venus. We didn't do so because the object of love was unobtainable, however, but because we saw Venusian relating as *more important* than Martial sexuality. And that's where we ran into trouble.

We might have noticed that the troubadours and Romantics seemed pretty unhappy much of the time. Yes, their unhappiness could drive them to ecstatic heights of blissful pining, but they seemed to prefer the rare time when they might actually have a few minutes of more earthly bliss with their partners. While it was very helpful to understand that love and sex were different, and that lusting for someone was not the same as loving them, problems can also result from the devaluation of sexuality and the placing of love in a more abstract, conceptual space.

Consider that it was the generation born with Neptune in the sign of Libra that was most active in reforming our ideas about relationship during the Uranus/Pluto in Libra era. The tendency to emphasize the Venusian side of relationship would have felt natural to this generation.

In practical terms, sexuality is important for relationships. The insight that it is not the *most important* factor should not be overextended to the point where sex is seen as unimportant. Sexual dissatisfaction is a common facet of many break-ups, as we know, and in the course of a separation understanding the fate of the energy of Mars is key to seeing how things will play out. For example, if the energy of Mars is diverted away from sexuality and into aggression, the break-up may be particularly nasty. On the other hand, if long-repressed sexual energy finds a new outlet, the urge to push the energy of Mars into aggression is less likely.

We often shy away for questions about sexuality during a break-up, probably because we assume that emotional and even practical issues are more important. We tacitly assume that other needs and other areas of life are more important at this sensitive time, and many people think it crude to be addressing sexuality at the time of a separation. But if sexuality played into the cause of the break-up and the drive energy is going to be used in one way or another during the separation process, then it is a mistake to ignore this powerful planet.

The following is a brief summary of how Mars in each element may approach sexuality within the context of the break-up of a relationship. As with any other astrological factor, bringing awareness and compassion to the process can greatly modify the way the energy manifests: all experiences are opportunities for growth.

With Mars in Fire signs (Aries, Leo, Sagittarius), there may be a tendency to move on quickly. These placements have a forward-directed energy that doesn't benefit from too much time in a holding pattern. Aries is the most likely to want to get back on the bicycle right away, as new beginnings are typically very reinforcing. Leo is the most likely to wait, as actions reflect on the self-image. Sagittarius enjoys exploring new possibilities, although even for Mars sex is just one aspect of this exploration.

If Mars is in an Air sign (Gemini, Libra, Aquarius), it focuses more on the social aspects of sexuality. Gemini is the Air sign most likely to espy some value in their new freedom and seek out new sexual experiences. Mars in Libra can be somewhat traditional with regard to sexuality, and may wait for the right circumstances or partner. In Aquarius, Mars is open to sex, but there is rarely a pressure around this area of life.

Water sign placements of Mars (Cancer, Scorpio, Pisces) are the most ambiguous, and sexuality is often very connected to emotions. Mars in Cancer is perhaps the most likely to retreat from sexuality during a break-up, with a need to direct energy inward for sorting out the emotions. Mars in Scorpio can bring out all of the self-protectiveness of this sign, and the focus on the relationship that is ending may overshadow the push to move on. With Mars in Pisces, there is a great deal of sexual and emotional energy blended (or tangled), so that it is more a matter of seeing how this will manifest over time in an individual. During break-ups, a Piscean Mars can be a monk (or nun) or a satyr (nymph).

Although you might expect that sensual Earth signs (Taurus, Virgo, Capricorn) are very sexual, during a break-up there is often very little pressure for sex. Taurus will typically enjoy whatever is available, but may displace pleasure into other areas of life. Mars can demonstrate why Virgo is the sign of the virgin, maintaining a distance from potential partners. Capricorn is often considered such a good placement for Mars because the raw drive of the planet is displaced into socially accepted goals, and this can certainly occur during the separation process, as the person throws themselves into work or maintaining their financial well being.

The placement of Mars will also say something about how the individual approaches the break-up itself. Fire signs may be the most ready to fight, while Mars in an Air sign may be more inclined to negotiate (although Aquarius may stand on principle). Water signs can drag out the process, maybe fighting over finances, as a way of processing emotional hurt. People with Mars in Earth signs can be very practical in the separation process, taking the attitude that things need not be overdramatized as long as they get what they need.

These brief summaries aren't meant to describe how someone with Mars in a given sign will act and react when a break-up occurs. They are intended as simple descriptions of the kinds of approaches that people may take during a separation. Understanding the basic energetic pattern of Mars is very helpful and will serve to put these summaries in context. Remember, also, that Mars is only part of the picture: Mars may be ready to move on quickly but the moon may not be. Individuals are complex.

Chapter 4
Venus

It goes without saying that Western astrologers will associate Venus with love and relationship. Although there are some excellent works suggesting that this planet has many meanings— even as the god (not goddess) of war when it appears as the morning star—our primary association of Venus is with love. In terms of chart analysis during a break-up, Venus can be thought of in this way.

Venus is one of the points that are very likely to be *affected* during a break-up. That is, it may be the *transited* planet, aspected by one of the outer planets. If that's the case, it of course helps to know as much as possible about Venus (and there have been volumes written on that already). Even if Venus isn't the transited planet, however, its position in a chart will still tell us a lot about the person's approach to relationship: what they want, need, expect, and offer in a partnership. It is those things that are being threatened, or at least reevaluated, when a relationship ends.

Although Venus is the planet we are most likely to think of in terms of partnership, it is really the moon that represents our

37

self-protective emotions and vulnerabilities, as well as our attachments to the past. For that reason, the moon is more likely to tell us how a person is feeling during a break-up. Venus, while not quite conceptual or abstract, is less visceral and describes *how* a person relates. It also says something about the partner, although the seventh house and its ruler usually say more about the specifics of significant partners.

Venus is very helpful for understanding how a person approaches relationship, what their assumptions about it may be, and what ideals they may hold dear. Exploring Venusian ideas and beliefs about relationships can be useful at any time, but during a break-up it is often very important. A good deal of suffering comes from holding onto assumptions that are inherited from society, family, and the media. The placement of Venus can tell us about both the natural, healthy expression of relationship energy as well as the limitations that are likely to be imposed on it.

In Fire signs, Venus usually indicates an outgoing, inspired approach to relationships. In Aries, there can be great joy in creating new relationships or in reinventing existing ones. In Leo, Venus likes to have fun and can really thrive on gestures of love. In Sagittarius, exploration is important, although there can also be a kind of stubborn clinging to ideas about how things should be. Although rebound relationships can be a problem, during break-ups the person with Venus in Fire signs usually does best if he or she can move on relatively quickly. Venus in Aries can accept the end as a matter of fact and begin looking towards the future quickly. Venus in Leo often feels slighted, and in Sagittarius there can be a sense that the partner was *wrong*.

In Air signs, Venus tends towards the more social aspects of relationship, and a certain amount of space around partnerships is not unusual. In Gemini, Venus often has a go-with-the-flow attitude that can be a little disconcerting for a partner with a more passionate view of relationship. Libra is perhaps the sign where Venus is most likely to cleave to a particular idea about what relationship should be, and in this sign tends towards the traditional. In Aquarius, Venus can also have very specific ideas about relationship, but they tend to be less traditional. Keep in mind that a person's ideas about tradition are often very local, inherited from family and the immediate environment, and not in any way a standard set of values and concepts (and certainly not *the astrologer's* ideas about traditional relationships!). In a break-up, Venus in Libra may want to follow the rules of separation. How difficult a separation is for Venus in Air signs depends on how tightly they cleave to a particular concept of relationship. Gemini usually has the easiest time adapting.

In Water signs, Venus emphasizes the feeling aspect of partnerships. In Cancer, the traditional aspects of relationship can be very prominent, and the need to share home and resources can be strong. In Scorpio, the intensity of the bond needs to be very strong, and its strength may be tested frequently. With Venus in Pisces, there is an appreciation of emotional connection, and at least the potential of a more open approach to partnership. In break-ups, Venus in Cancer and Scorpio can have a very difficult time, because security needs have been entangled with relationship. As is typical for the sign of the fish, Venus in Pisces can respond by either casual acceptance of the end or extremes of loss and pain. Remember, though, that what is affected is mostly how the person relates—look to the moon for the more basic emotional response.

In Earth signs, Venus has a direct, sensual approach to relationship. It isn't that Venus is just lounging around enjoying things, but rather that things are taken in a one-step-at-a-time way. In Taurus, Venus tends to be confident in the ability to relate, while in Virgo that confidence is often lacking. You'll hear a lot about Venus in Virgo being too picky where partners are concerned, and that can happen. However, what you are most likely to see is that the person with Venus in Virgo seeks to serve the partner and be helpful and supportive, often as a means of demonstrating their worth. In Capricorn, practical aspects of relationship can dominate. In separations, Venus in Earth signs often manages relatively well, although Virgo can be concerned about future relationship potential ("no one will ever love me again!"). Taurus and Capricorn tend not to be very pressured about the future of relationship (Taurus because it is assumed, Capricorn because it is not imperative).

Once again, although Venus is in a sense *the* relationship planet, it signifies how a person will relate, and is not necessarily the most important planet in terms of inner experience. It is also much easier to bring awareness to the functioning of Venus than to the moon or sun, which are more primary to the person.

Each element has one sign that tends towards a more traditional, protective, and cautious approach to relationship (and sometimes rigidity). Cancer, Libra, Sagittarius, and Capricorn can often benefit from being gently pried loose from their ideas about how relationship has to be. We might throw Aquarius into this group, too. An understanding that their partnership needs can be met without the relationship taking a specific form can be liberating for these signs.

Venus in Hard Aspect to the Outer Planets in the Natal Chart

Although in later chapters we will discuss relationships that are colored by the outer planets, Venus in a hard aspect (conjunction, square, or opposition) to the outer planets has a special role in creating the attitudes a person has towards relationship. For that reason, it's beneficial to list a few specific possibilities.

Venus and Saturn

When Venus is in hard aspect to Saturn in the natal chart, there is often a kind of depression around the area of relationships. Rather than being an active sort of sadness, it is more a kind of tacit acceptance of the limitations of relationship. The person may feel that relationship is just not their thing, or that they are unlovable, or that they cannot be with the people they love. While some hardship in the area of relationship is indeed likely (it is for everyone, after all), the depressed attitude around this area of life is not entirely realistic. With maturity, the person has the ability to build solid relationships, usually after the Saturn return at age 29 – 30 years. Still, if a break-up occurs, there is a tendency to feel that the relationship life is over—an exaggeration of legitimate sadness. Challenging the person about whether his or her doom and gloom approach to the future of relationship is *really* realistic is often very helpful.

Venus and Uranus

Here we have almost the opposite energy of Venus with Saturn. When Uranus is aspecting Venus in the natal chart, we may find that a strong independence is at work in relationship, and traditional ideas about partnership hold little sway with the person. If the sign positions work out reasonably well—let's say Venus in Pisces squared by Uranus in Sagittarius—then it is likely that little conflict is present within the person. If the signs indicate a more traditional approach on the part of Venus— perhaps Venus in Libra squared by Uranus in Capricorn—then there may be internal conflict as the person needs to resolve a tendency towards conventional relationships with a personal inclination for more inventive approaches.

Within relationships, the person with Venus/Uranus may have a strong need for time alone, or a need to pursue career or creative projects without the partner. It may also be the case, particularly with the opposition, that it is the partner who needs his or her own time and space. Again, if Venus is well disposed to creative relationship patterns—Venus in Aquarius opposed by Uranus in Leo—then it should not be too difficult to work things out. Venus in more self-concerned Leo opposed by Uranus in Aquarius could be more challenging.

In a break-up situation, Venus/Uranus may be quick to leave, and usually will not have a great deal of patience to stay in a failing relationship. However, if the partner leaves out of the blue (again, more likely with an opposition), the person may feel shattered by the loss of the relationship. Although there is usually a great deal of adaptability when Venus/Uranus is part of someone's chart, we shouldn't assume that they welcome or even accept change easily. Once again, it is the moon that is most likely to describe a person's inner response to a break-up, while Venus is more involved in the styles of relating.

Venus and Neptune

This is a very sensitive cosmic equation. The combination of Venus and Neptune can create an empathic absorption with the partner, and/or an all-or-nothing attitude that swings between the heights of ecstasy and the depths of despair. At best, Venus/Neptune can move relationship beyond the limits of personal interaction and into the realm of the spiritual, while at worst it can mean clingy codependence. It's a tricky one.

When a separation occurs, the person with Venus/Neptune may react very deeply. If there is a powerful connection between these planets in the natal chart, then any of the manifestations that transiting Neptune can bring about (see Chapter 9) may occur. While Venus/Saturn may have a cold acceptance of being alone again, Venus/Neptune often has an active kind of despair. The need to be grounded is especially strong for these folks when break-ups occur, and some attention to daily routine can be encouraged. At the same time, a look in the other direction to spiritual practice is also often very helpful.

Venus and Pluto

The profound intensity of Pluto does not have a very good reputation in combination with Venus, but that is largely a matter of perspective. Relationships go deep when these two planets are in a significant aspect to each other, and indeed that can mean difficulty. But it can also mean that there is a potential for profound transformation through partnerships, and that it is through relating with others that the person learns to connect with his or her own deepest soul level. Limiting ideas, fantasies, societal rules, family expectations, and many other things that we incorporate into our relationships will all need to be stripped

42

away before the full potential of Venus/Pluto can emerge, but when it does, the connection is very deep.

For a person with such potential for deep connection, the loss of a relationship can be very traumatic. Even if at some level there is the awareness that the partnership was not strong enough, there is still likely to be some resistance to the idea of walking away from it. There can be a tendency to hang on, or dig in, to prevent the partner from going until every last drop of passion (and anger is a passion!) has been wrung from the relationship.

These few ideas should help to orient you to Venus in aspect to the outer planets in the natal chart, and how these configurations are activated during a break-up. There are no hard-and-fast rules, and many factors affect how people handle changes in their lives. However, at times of stressful transitions it is not unusual to find ourselves moving into old routines (and ruts), so these patterns may be more likely to emerge during separations than when a relationship is going well. As always, it is very much a matter of individual awareness and experience, and the astrologer needs to talk to the client to know where they are within the break-up process.

Chapter 5
Relationship Patterns

Relationship Patterns and Break-ups

Many astrologers have some means of assessing a birth chart in a general way. We may look at East-West orientation, Marc Edmund Jones' chart patterns, the distribution of the elements and modes (and chart signature), and so on. A similar approach is helpful in chart comparisons and relationship consultations. An overview of the relationship dynamics on a macro level can provide a context for the more specific aspects and interactions we see among the planets and houses.

When it comes to the ending of a relationship, it is often the case that these larger macro-level patterns have a lot to say about why things are no longer working. The following patterns can help you to understand both the potential and challenges of a partnership. Keep in mind that any relationship is a dynamic process, and what is an opportunity at one time can become a stress at another, and vice-versa. Also, as with chart patterns and other techniques, be aware that textbook examples are relatively rare in real life and many relationships show a blending of more than one pattern.

General Patterns

Complementary Relationships

Opposites attract, we've been told, and sometimes they do. Astrologically, a complementary relationship is one in which each person brings something that is lacking in the partner's chart, or in opposition to the partner's energy.

Often, this is seen in the elemental balance, particularly when someone has a large number of planets in one element, or very few or no planets in an element. It is most common for each partner to balance the elemental emphasis of the other. For example, Bill may have very little Air in his chart, while Doug has six planets in Air signs. Since he has so many planets in Air, Doug is low on other elements – say Water and Fire – which Bill has in quantity. If we look at the twenty planets between the two of them, the elemental balance is even: something like five planets in each of the four elements. The relationship is complimentary in terms of elements.

We might think that people who lack an element will have no real concern for what that element signifies, but it is just as often the case that they will be very tuned into the element's energy— although often in an awkward way. For example, someone with no planets in Earth might indeed be unconcerned about money and material things, but it is also quite likely that they will be very focused on finances and possessions. It's not a lack of *interest*, but a lack of *perspective* that tends to be the problem for someone with relatively few planets in an element. Sometimes, people with no Earth wind up being true misers. Because they are never really comfortable with the material world, they obsess over it. The opposite may also be true, someone with a lot of Earth in their chart may take the material world for granted and be unconcerned about money, assuming that it will always be there. In a complimentary relationship, the partner can thus be a source of fascination, because they display ease in dealing with things that the person finds so alien.

Complementary relationships can also be seen in the distribution of planets. For example, one person may have most of their planets above the horizon or on the Eastern side of the chart, while the partner has the opposite. Another possibility is that a particularly strong planet in the chart—say the sun or moon—may be in the sign opposite the same planet in the partner's chart.

Another facet of complementary relationships is seen the charged/neutral distinction that Eric Meyers introduced in his book, *Elements and Evolution*. Eric pointed out that the Fire and Water elements are *charged*, that is they are emotional, opinionated, and associated with desire; while Earth and Air are *neutral*, pertaining to structure or information and lacking in subjective content. In relationships, we can see that someone with strong charged energy can bring passion to a partner with a more neutral profile, while the partner with a neutral emphasis can provide expansion, structure, and context to the more charged person.

The strength of complementary relationships is that they provide a kind of dynamic balance. It's not that the partners' planets zero out to a perfect equality, but rather that each partner keeps giving something of what the other lacks. It's exciting, among other things, because each partner is continually exposed to a very different approach to life.

That different approach, however, can wind up grating on the nerves after a while. The person with a Cancer moon would like to retreat into his shell from time to time, while his Capricorn moon partner is always ready for the next project. He thinks she needs to rest and wind down, she thinks he is lazy. An Earth-heavy partner is always ready to splurge and enjoy a nice dinner out, while her Earth-light partner is constantly wondering where the money is coming from.

In break-ups, complementary relationships tend to show a kind of repulsion that is equal in force (but opposite in direction) to the initial attraction. There is often a sense of having had enough of the different perspective the partner had to offer.

Supplementary Relationships

Supplementary relationships are those in which the charts of the partners add to each other, emphasizing a quality that is present in both of their charts. This relationship pattern has several flavors.

The most basic form of supplementary relationship occurs when the two partners directly reinforce a basic quality in each other's charts. For instance, the sun of one partner falls near the ascendant of the other. The sun person helps to energize the ascendant person's life, adding vitality. The ascendant person expresses the sun person's solar energy in a very direct way.

A variation occurs when there are challenging aspects involved in an area of one partners' chart. One of my first clues to the validity of astrology came from exploring this phenomenon. I am a Leo, and my sun is in a close, approaching opposition to Saturn—who is always ready to cool off some of my fiery solar energy. Beginning in high school, I dated or was very attracted to four young women, all of which were also Leos (in fact, their birthdays were all within the second decanate of the sign). I was seeking their fiery Leo suns as a means of supplementing my own solar energy. While the first variation of supplementary relationships simply adds two harmonious factors, this manifestation is more about lending support.

Another possibility is that the two partners share the same challenging aspect, or some variation of it. For example, she has Mars opposite Saturn, and he has a Mars-Saturn conjunction. They are both working on a similar theme in their charts, and so they tend to support each other's work. This is not necessarily a very harmonious variation of supplementary relationships, but it can help a great deal to be with someone who is working out similar issues.

It can happen that one partner offers support to a planet under stress. For example, she has the moon in Sagittarius conjunct

Pluto, while his Jupiter in Leo is trine to her moon. In a truly supplementary relationship, she will in some way offer a similar bit of support to some factor in his chart. In this example, her Pluto is trine to his Jupiter.

Supplementary relationships are very reinforcing and the bonds can go quite deep. In many ways, they *feel* right, as it is generally the case that both partners speak the same emotional language. However, after a time it is to be hoped that each partner will be able to work with the chart's energy without the support of the partner. When she finally gets a handle on that Mars-Saturn opposition, she doesn't need him around to find new ways to work on the same issues. When a person comes into his or her own and can express their sun sign more directly, there is less need for another to show the solar qualities via their ascendant. It can certainly be the case that supplementary relationships show life-long harmony, but it can also happen that once a person gets on their own feet, they no longer feel the need for a crutch. Because of the deep connection and support that these relationships tend to offer, break-ups can be very emotionally difficult.

Catalytic Relationships

If you look at two charts and say, "Oh, no, they shouldn't be together," you are probably looking at a catalytic relationship (and you may very well be wrong). These relationships often have significant squares between the partners' charts, and often to planets that are already under some form of stress in the natal charts. Unlike the supportive nature of supplementary relationships, in catalytic partnerships the partner's aspects may seem to make things *more* stressful. For example, Mary has her moon in Scorpio square to Saturn, while Jeanine has her Pluto conjunct Mary's moon. Or it could be as simple as two people with their suns square to each other. Sometimes, an unaspected planet in one partner's chart is really lit up by the other partner's planets. Fire and Water, the two charged elements, can sometimes indicate a catalytic relationship, as when one partner has a lot of

Fire and the other an abundance of Water: what *could* be a complementary relationship can be challenging to the point of being catalytic.

Catalytic relationships help to catalyze change. They bring to full manifestation areas of the chart that may be challenging but unconscious or otherwise not dealt with productively. Catalytic relationship patterns seem to say, "you've got to work with this, and you've got to work with it now." They're not always fun, but these relationships can be very productive. When the work is over, however, there may be little to hold these partnerships together.

Karmic Relationships

Relationships that involve key planets aspecting the nodes of the moon, the angles, the vertex, and/or the 12th house often have a karmic component to them. The lunar nodes are particularly important, and a partner's planets conjunct the nodes can indicate a very strong karmic attachment.

Now, when we start talking about karma and past lives, we seem to be heading into a land of mystery. Ideas about love surviving through the ages come to mind, and sometimes that may be what is going on. What we know—and all we really know through astrology—is that there is a strong connection between these souls and they have some work to do here together in this lifetime. The specifics of the nodal aspects and planets involved can give us a clue about the nature of the work and the potential for relationship in this incarnation. However, there are a few caveats to keep in mind.

The first is that karmic relationships are powerful regardless of their specific form, and we tend to lack the language and concepts to understand strong bonds in anything other than romantic terms. In other words, when we meet someone to whom we have a karmic attachment, we tend to really feel very strongly about the person, and somehow we just know this person is very important to us, and that there is a strange, uncanny quality to the relationship. The thing is, it isn't necessarily love, at least not in the sense of romantic love. We don't have too many ways of interpreting strong, mystical feelings for another person, however, so we tend to feel we are in love with them.

Even when there truly is a romantic relationship, karmic bonds often mean only that we are saying "hi!" to the person in this lifetime. Yes, we are affirming our soul connection with them, and we recognize that this is a profoundly important relationship in our lives. Yet the mystical, ecstatic qualities of these connections often don't translate very well into partnerships of the "who's turn is it to do the food shopping?" variety. In other words, the relationship may be a bit too deep to function on a more mundane level. The key to understanding karmic relationships is that their real purpose is to acknowledge and bring to consciousness the connection. It is rarely the case that there is anything much to *do* beyond that, which is the irony of the timeless quality of these partnerships.

It is very common for these relationships to never really get off the ground, but sometimes they do. In either case, there may be a need to work out issues that have been on the table for lifetimes, although there probably isn't a great pressure to complete the work, only to make progress. In any event, for the purpose of this book on break-ups, the point is that the relationship will tend to stay together until they have accomplished whatever task they set out to do in this go-round. Once that task is done, however, the soul mates are often on their separate ways, usually without too much doubt or regret, although there is usually a lingering sense of importance about the relationship.

Outer Planet Patterns

While the general relationship patterns outlined above are useful in providing some background to help understand the dynamics of a break-up, the core of this book deals with the patterns set by the outer planets. While the transits of Saturn, Uranus, Neptune, and Pluto are going to be used to describe the overall patterns of separation, those same planets tend to influence relationships apart from break-ups.

50

In other words, relationships are colored in a Saturnian, Uranian, Neptunian, or Plutonian light. To complicate matters a bit, the relationship pattern may or may not match the break-up pattern, so that a Saturnian relationship may dissolve under a Neptunian transit. And to make things even more complex, each partner may have a different outer planet that colors their individual relationship picture.

If one partner has a Saturnian view of relationship while the other has a Neptunian view, and they get together to form a Uranian relationship that ends under a Pluto transit, is there any point in bothering to look at relationship patterns at all? It seems a bit like we may be throwing in everything but the kitchen sink and diluting the value of any one piece of information.

That would be true if we were looking for the one "real" reason for a break-up, if we were being astro-detectives focused on the clues that led to the end of a partnership. What we are really doing, however, is not looking for objective facts but for *perspective*. If one partner has a Saturnian view of relationship, they will experience a Uranian relationship and also a Plutonian break-up from that perspective. Their Neptunian partner will also be going through the Uranian relationship and Plutonian break-up, but they will see it very differently. It is like two people on different sides of the same statue—they each see the same thing, but from different perspectives.

It is this *seeing the same thing from different angles* that causes so much distress in relationships of all kinds. We don't necessarily disagree about objective facts, but we each filter them through a unique lens that frames the meaning of the data. A partner with a Uranian view of relationship may take freedom for granted, while her Saturnian partner feels threatened when the couple spends time apart from each other. There isn't necessarily any question about how much they are together and apart, but rather about the *meaning* of those quantities of time. As astrologers, we can gain some insight into each partners' perspective, and that can help to illuminate the situation.

51

What do we look for to determine an outer planet relationship pattern? For each partner, we would look to the usual suspects: Venus, the seventh house and its ruler, and the sun and moon (within the contexts I've described earlier). To an extent, the ascendant also says something about relationship, because it describes the person's most immediate approach to life. That is, for example, someone with a Scorpio ascendant will have a somewhat Plutonian approach to *everything*, including relationship. Look for these points to be in signs associated (or ruled by) the outer planets, and close aspects between the points and the outer planets. Outer planets in the seventh house also suggest a strong influence on partnership.

As you know (or will know!), astrology is rarely as simple as our explanations suggest. When you actually look at a chart, you may find a great deal of information that makes an assessment of the outer planet character of the relationship complex. A client has Scorpio on the seventh house cusp, suggesting a Plutonian approach to relationship. Yet she also has Uranus (in the sign of Scorpio) in the seventh, close to the descendent, and Venus in Aquarius. Is her approach to relationship Uranian? Plutonian?

To answer questions like that, we have to assume that both potentialities exist, and that they may both shape relationships to some extent. In talking with the person, we can begin to see how each planet functions in actual partnerships thus far in life. In this example, despite herself the woman has had a series of relationships with partners she feels are not the type of person she would/should be with. They break with her expectations, in that they come from diverse cultures, which is a problem for her. It is easy to see that there is a strong Uranian component to her relationships, yet we can also notice that she continues to have these relationships that are in a way transforming (Pluto) her view of relationship. You don't have to settle on simple and simplistic answers: allow the complexity to flow through your interpretations.

An important factor is the transits the person was having at the time the relationship formed. For example, a man who finds a partner and marries when Saturn moves into his seventh house will have a Saturnian pattern for at least that relationship. In the case of slower moving outer planets, you may see that relationships begin and end over the course of the same extended transit.

When looking at the partnership itself, one can use the composite chart and synastry to find the dominant outer planet relationship. Strong connections between one partner's Venus and the other's Neptune would begin to suggest a Neptunian relationship, at least from the perspective of the Venusian partner. A composite conjunction of Venus to Saturn, or Saturn in the first house of the composite chart, would suggest a Saturnian relationship. We'll explore the various relationship types in depth with various examples later in the book.

Finally, the chart for the beginning of the relationship is important, if it can be obtained with any reasonable accuracy. It is at least helpful to know the position of Saturn and the outer planets at the time the relationship formed, as we can then see transits at later times, particularly the cycle of the planets to themselves. Once in a while, a client remembers the actual time of the first meeting, and that chart has a great deal of value in understanding the overall relationship pattern.

One thing that may bother astrologers a little is my insistence on using one of the four outer planets to characterize a relationship. Suppose that a person has Venus in Sagittarius, with Jupiter in Leo on the seventh house cusp. Would it not be appropriate to say that this person has a Jupiterian approach to relationship?

Not for our purposes. I agree that the beneficent handprint of Jupiter will probably be all over this person's partnerships, of course, and we shouldn't discount Jupiter when considering relationship patterns. It is similarly possible to consider solar, lunar, Venusian, or Martial approaches to partnership in many contexts. But when we are looking at break-ups, the emphasis needs to be on Saturn or one of the transpersonal planets.

Essentially, you are within the sphere of Saturn, or beyond it. As much as Jupiter or any other planet within Saturn's orbit may affect relationship, they are still within the context of Saturnian rules and boundaries. Jupiter or Venus may give a different tone to partnerships than, say, Mars, but all of them will answer to Saturn's expectations. Within Saturnian boundaries, there are assumptions about they way things should be, and a sense of limitation as to what is possible. A strong Venus can mean those assumptions are harmonious and palatable, a strong Jupiter may mean that the rules are bent a bit with a wink and a smile, and so on. But the basic assumption of the rules and expectations is still there. Those *musts* and *shoulds* vary by culture, family, religion, and many other factors, but for each person or relationship they are seen as real.

For those persons and relationships with an emphasis beyond the Saturnian realm, there are a few possibilities. Particularly since the dramatic shifts in relationship that took place during the 1960's and 70's, many people are comfortable charting their own course in partnership, and Saturn's expectations bind them temporarily if at all. Generations born since 1980 tend to be especially free in matters of relationship.

However, many people go beyond the rings of Saturn with hesitation and fear. While they may be called upon to revolutionize, dissolve, and uproot our traditional expectations about relationship, they don't necessarily see that as an easy task or one they want. A standard, 1950's style partnership may not be something they are likely to find, but it doesn't mean they don't keep a wistful eye on that image. Again, during a break-up, the emphasis is going to be on the outer planets, and Saturn is the default outer planet if none of the others seems to dominate the picture.

Saturnian Relationships: It Is What It Is

Saturnian partnerships are the least reflective of any of the relationship patterns. As I've said, the Saturnian pattern is the default relationship type, and until fairly recently it was more or less the only kind of relationship there was. Like Saturn, these partnerships are bound by a sense of duty and obligation, and by a respect for the rules. In the old days—and in some places, still—

arranged marriages were the epitome of Saturnian relationships: the family decided what was good for you (and them) and made the decision for you. The weighty divorce laws that have finally given way over the past few decades are another example of Saturn venturing into the area of relationship. There will be more to say about Saturn and the history of relationships in a later chapter, but when you think of rules, written or unwritten, dominating a partnership, think of the planet with the rings.

In a Saturnian relationship, there is a strong tendency to maintain the status quo, and the relationship is solidified by reluctance to change and a tacit acceptance of the way things are. If they survive, Saturnian relationships tend to get better with age, as all things Saturnian and Capricornian do, but they are not usually a lot of fun. Drama is missing from these partnerships, by and large, and it is often the case that the couple appears as though they have been married for years—even when they are still dating.

Saturn also requires a decision, and these relationships always start with someone making a choice, although that decision may be many years in the past. That a trade-off may be involved is also part of the Saturnian pattern, and it is not unusual to hear stories of how this partnership is one of compromise—"I was in love with someone before, really in love, but I knew it couldn't work...Bob gives me the stability I need...."

One challenge of a Saturnian relationship is to maintain vitality, to keep the partnership from becoming crusty and inflexible. Fear goes wherever Saturn puts his boot prints, and change can be a source of anxiety when this relationship pattern prevails. Another challenge is to learn to define the relationship in terms that both partners create and agree upon, rather than slipping into unconscious acceptance of society's expectations.

The rewards of a Saturnian partnership are slow in coming in many cases, but they are real. On a material level, there is often a real and deep knowledge that the other person is there for you through thick and thin. Saturn is all about "'til death do us part" in most cases, although this book is full of exceptions. On a spiritual level, Saturnian relationships tend to be those where we do real work, resolving karmic issues and developing our personalities. The karmic issues aren't necessarily between the two people in the sense of a past life relationship. Rather, each person is well suited to be the other's teacher in this life, helping to work out his or her individual karma (in a sense, all issues are karmic). Saturn demands maturity, and maturity is something many of us leave at the door when it comes to relationship. Think about it: how much easier is it to tantrum over love than career and other aspects of life? With a strong Saturnian edge to the partnership, we are called to learn the lessons of maturity.

Individuals with Saturnian relationship tendencies may have Capricorn on the seventh house or rising (a Capricorn ascendant give traditional Cancer on the seventh house cusp); Venus, the moon, or the sun in Capricorn; or those planets or the ruler of the seventh in a hard aspect to Saturn. Aspects to Venus affect relationship most directly, of course, but don't discount the way relationship can be affected along with everything else when the sun or moon is in conjunction, square, or opposition to Saturn.

In the relationship itself, you would look for the same things in the composite chart, along with Saturn rising or on the midheaven. Aspects to Saturn in synastry are another indication of this relationship pattern.

Uranian Relationships: Shake, Rattle, and Roll

Uranus is the first transpersonal planet we are going to consider in relationships and break-ups, and in many ways it is the easiest to understand. Uranus offers the transcendence of Saturnian reality and the ability to go beyond the rules of Saturn's realm. Uranus allows us to chart our own course, to express and assert our individuality. Uranus has the reputation of being a disruptive planet, but that is only true if we assume a Saturnian perspective where maintaining the status quo is the top priority. Saturn represents authority and tradition, and these are—at least at first—found externally, in priests and rabbis, parents and teachers, and the many written and unwritten rules of society. At some point, however, we can begin to internalize Saturnian

56

authority and take responsibility for ourselves. We are then ready for Uranus.

As with Neptune and Pluto, Uranus is paradoxically both very personal and transpersonal in its focus. Wherever we experience Uranus, we find that we break the mold of conventionality, and upturn the expectations of family, friends, society, and even ourselves. Yet as much as this is our personal task, we are assigned it in order to help transform our culture—it is as if we are given a mission by the Cosmos to lead by example. While the potential of Uranus is very liberating, we need to keep in mind that not everyone craves freedom, especially in the area of relationships, so that we often see people rebelling against the rebellious energy of this planet.

Applied to relationships, the energy of Uranus manifests in several ways. One typical manifestation is in the choice of partners, who are often quite different than what we would expect. Ethnicity, socioeconomic status, and gender are obvious choices for different-than-expected partners, but there is really no end to the possibilities.

Another way that a Uranian influence can be seen on relationships is in the amount of freedom required by one, or both, partners. A strong Uranus often means that both partners need to feel free to pursue their own agenda, and awareness that although relationship is important, it isn't necessarily primary. A "hold on loosely, but don't let go" attitude (as 38 Special put it) is usually the best formula for Uranian relationships.

A third possibility often stems from the first two, and that is a novel relationship pattern. Long-distance relationships, not living together even after years of partnership, and open and semi-open relationships are examples, but this list is just a start. Remember that what is novel or even unusual in one culture may be quite typical in another, and this needs to be taken into account.

Uranian relationships are seen when the planet Uranus is present in or rules the seventh house, or is in aspect to Venus. An Aquarius emphasis in relationship points and planets also suggests the influence of Uranus. In a composite chart, an angular

Uranus also needs to be considered as a dominant theme in the partnership.

Neptunian Relationships: Is That All There Is?

Applied to any area of life, the energy of Neptune is usually hard to describe. That's because Neptune is primarily about *other realities*, those that are far from our mundane concerns. Neptune connects us to feelings and images that are beyond our experience of the physical world, and trying to map those onto our everyday reality inevitably involves some serious adjustments—it's like trying to draw three-dimensional objects in two-dimensional space. That becomes even more apparent when the area in question is relationships, because romance is one of the few areas where we in the contemporary Western world still allow ourselves access to the mysterious.

Think about it: in what other area of life is it acceptable to talk about things as being fated? How often in our culture do we hear the word *soul* without it being embedded in the term *soul mate*? Take a rational, hard-boiled business school graduate who thumbs his or her nose at the mention of spirituality, astrology, and anything beyond the physical world, and then listen to this person when they fall in love. Suddenly things are magical, meant to be, and enchanted. Romance is where we most easily let Neptune into our lives.

It is common astrological lore that Neptune rarely delivers to the mundane realm all that it promises. Neptune shows us unlimited potential, but we often find ourselves walking away with a very limited reality. When we try to bring the promise of Neptune down into the Saturnian realm of concrete reality, the grand image dissolves in the process. We may hold on with sentimental longing for that brief moment when everything seemed possible, and we can try to recreate the high with drugs or drama, but in the end we may feel that we have lost touch with the source of our inspiration. This can be all the more acute when the area in question is partnership.

A Neptunian relationship pattern isn't necessarily difficult or painful, but it does suggest that the person needs to have a great deal or awareness in order to avoid the pitfalls of Neptune. At its best, Neptune helps us to say "yes" to experience without holding on to expectations. We are ready to take the experience for what it offers on its own terms. Let the ego take a back seat, with *shoulds* and *musts* in the trunk and "I want" dropped off at the nearest bus stop, and Neptune can show us how loving another person really is a spiritual path.

That can be hard to do! The danger of a Neptunian relationship pattern is an over-idealization of the partner or the relationship itself. There can be something about these relationships that continue to draw a person towards them, even after they have gone sour or ended completely. In fact, in terms of break-ups, it is very possible that a Neptunian relationship will take a long time to end, as someone does not want to let go. Even after the relationship is over, there can be an extended period of mourning for the loss, and often years (and subsequent relationships) pass and there is still a sense of loss and *if only*.

Neptunian relationship patterns not only include an inflated view of partnerships that have an actual history, but also unrequited love and instances where the desired partner is unavailable for one reason or another. In these instances, it is often as if the mere potential of the relationship causes as much of a sense of loss as a relationship that actually existed. Under a Neptune transit, a young woman met a man while she was studying abroad for a semester, and she grew very attached to him. Although they had no real romantic relationship, in many ways she considers him the love of her life. Years later she lamented, "I just don't understand how this relationship did not happen." In a sense, of course, it did happen, but that sense is Neptunian: experiential and spiritual.

One additional idea is worth keeping in mind when Neptune colors a partnership, although you may not want to share this with the client in all circumstances. Neptunian relationships often feel very much like past life connections. Sometimes, that does seem to be the case, especially when there are also nodal aspects, but at other times it may be more likely that the otherworldliness of the relationship simply opens the person to the possibility of past lives. This needs to be evaluated and decided upon on a case-by-case basis, but be aware that there are often strong feelings around this possibility.

Plutonian Relationships: Going Deep

Despite the eye rolling of astrologers, Plutonian relationships are not necessarily difficult. They are deep, and they require an extraordinary amount of openness and honesty, but they aren't necessarily difficult. In fact, the depth of Plutonian connections can be powerful enough to make many typical relationship issues appear as mere trifles.

Pluto is about transformation, about death and rebirth. When a Plutonian pattern is apparent in a person's chart in the area of relationship, it is usually the case that they will be transformed by their relationships. They will be challenged by their partnerships, and they can truly evolve into more whole beings if they can successfully meet these challenges. The key is often learning to let go, to allow the process of being reinvented without controlling it.

As you probably know, there is also a more difficult side to Pluto, and that emerges around the question of *control*. When Pluto is strong, processes seek to transform the ego, but the ego often has ideas of its own and thinks that power is there for its own use. When control enters into relationships, the usual suspects emerge: jealousy, emotional manipulation, and anger. When these more difficult sides to Pluto are apparent, a good strategy (but not an easy one!) is to work to get the person to see their partner's perspective. Pluto, coopted for the ego's purposes, can be remarkably black-and-white in its thinking and feeling, and the introduction of gradation and multiple perspectives can be very helpful.

It is important to keep in mind that Pluto ultimately follows its own agenda. While people may feel like they have the Plutonian power, ultimately it has them. The ego can pump itself up and push through a number of situations, but the real power resides in the transformative process itself—the ego often finds out that it was creating a tempest in a tea cup, and all its machinations amount to very little in the end. Helping clients to see the bigger picture is crucial when they are into the darker side of Plutonian energy.

Even when Plutonian relationships are at their best, people often feel a bit uneasy, recognizing that they are getting into something that goes beyond their ego's sense of control. One client demonstrated a very Plutonian relationship pattern. She had the sun in Scorpio in the seventh house, and her fiancé had his moon in Scorpio close to his midheaven. They had met (she recalled the exact place and time, a Plutonian after-work meeting at a bar) with Pluto on the IC, and she had planned their wedding with Pluto in the first house, three degrees away from the ascendant. She had reservations about the relationship, and in fact about the man she was going to marry. But she said that she felt she had to go through with the marriage, to see what would happen. Although we can question the wisdom of entering into a serious commitment while still very unsure of the relationship, I also think we can appreciate that her attitude was appropriate for a Plutonian partnership in that she was already acknowledging that she did not have all of the control, that she was part of a process that was in a sense larger than her personal ideas. Yet she was no victim—she knew that she could leave the relationship if she needed to. Maintaining a balance between surrender and control is difficult, but key to avoiding becoming a victim in Plutonian circumstances.

Chapter 6
Timing

Timing is one of the most important aspects of astrology, and in a sense astrology is about the relation of time to meaning. When it comes to the ending of a relationship, the more we understand about the timing, the deeper we can go in comprehending the dynamics that are at work. Once again, I have to remind you that we are using timing to understand rather than predict a break-up, and any of the things discussed in this chapter can and do happen within the context of relationships that continue to survive and thrive.

Most of the things we'll cover in this chapter are relevant to each of the four outer planets, although of course the timing is different for each: Saturn transits generally last about nine months, while Pluto transits can go on for years, for example. Because the duration of transits (and progressions) can be extended, it is not unusual to have more than one operative during the break-up. For instance, a couple may begin to have issues as Saturn transits their composite Venus, and as that transit ends we find that Uranus is aspecting one of the partner's seventh house. Specific timing considerations for each of the four outer planets are discussed in the relevant chapters.

Rather than trying to zero in exclusively on the most active aspect at the moment, it is usually a better strategy to create a narrative based on the relevant transits, extending back in time to the first stressful aspect. I often find it helpful to relate the transits that are describing the end of the relationship to the ones that were present at the beginning. At times, there will be an obvious harmony between the two sets (e.g., Uranus trine Venus at the start of the relationship, but Uranus square Venus at the end), while at other times the two sets of transits look very different (Saturn inaugurates the relationship, Neptune dissolves it).

Sometimes a planet has its fingerprints all over a relationship. A woman with Saturn conjunct Venus in her natal chart marries a man with a Capricorn moon, Saturn is on the midheaven of their composite chart, and the relationship ends after 14 years (half a Saturn cycle). When you see things like that, it is helpful to explicitly state the lessons and potentials of Saturn, because it has characterized the entire relationship. When the planet most closely associated with the break-up is not closely associated with the overall relationship pattern (or the pattern of one of the partners), then it is usually a matter of incorporating a new perspective on relationship. Thus, the Saturnian couple who experiences a Uranian break-up may be called beyond the rules and formalities of the Saturnian style of relating, while a couple with a very Neptunian partnership may need to learn to incorporate the more grounded energy of Saturn in future relationships.

Astrologers work with a lot of information: ten planets, the angles, the nodes of the moon, house cusps, aspects, and perhaps asteroids, fixed stars, minor aspects, hypothetical planets, declination, tertiary progressions, and a catalog of other heavenly bodies, points, techniques, and systems. So, it makes sense that we try to simplify—we can't possibly process all the information, and we certainly cannot expect our clients to do even a small part of what we do. When it comes to relationships, the need for simplicity is greater, in the sense that there are more charts to consider. Yet it really isn't possible to condense all of the relevant information down to one single statement. Using a narrative approach that encompasses the dispositions of each partner, the relationship's beginnings, and the stages of its ending allows us to present the story in a meaningful and coherent way, without reducing it to a one-dimensional pronouncement.

As we go through the following transits and progressions, remember that relationships and their endings are complex, and it is usually better to acknowledge the importance of "this *and* that" rather than trying to sort out whether "this *or* that" has the most significance. The various aspects are presented in order of obviousness, not necessarily power: it is easy to see how Venus corresponds to relationship, but that doesn't mean that a transit to Venus is always the most significant in a separation.

A Word About Orbs

In general, the approaching orb of a transit (the time before the transiting planet hits the relevant transited point in the chart) is determined by the speed of the transiting planet. Saturn moves fastest among the outer planets, so we use a larger orb. Pluto moves slowly, so it makes sense to use a smaller orb, as it may take a year or more for Pluto to traverse even a few degrees. The orbs I usually use for approaching transits are:
>Saturn: 10 degrees
>Uranus: 8 degrees
>Neptune: 7 degrees
>Pluto: 6 degrees

However, you need to take into account things like retrograde motion and planetary speed. So, if Saturn gets within 9 degrees of Venus then retrogrades out of the 10-degree range for most of the next six months, I wouldn't expect too much to be happening until it gets into and stays within the 10-degree area. Pluto has a highly irregular orbit, so that during its time in Scorpio it was moving rather fast and so could have a larger orb, while it is currently slowing and the orb may need to be decreased.

Practically speaking, for most transit work, I look to the time about six to eight months before the first exact hit of the transit, thus I use orbs based on *time* rather than *distance*. I would add, however, that as soon as an outer planet enters the sign of the transited planet (this works especially well with conjunctions), there is often a noticeable rumbling in the area of life signified by the transited planet. Conversely, I find that approaching aspects need a smaller orb when they are out of sign.

The work we do when working with break-ups reframes the orb question. Because we are not predicting separations but illuminating their meaning, we can expect that at least some of the relevant transits are underway or even in the past. However, it is also true that the narrative of the break-up may continue well beyond the time of the consultation with the astrologer, so it may be necessary to look to future transits and the timing of the next stages of the relationship.

Separating orbs are usually much smaller. Two degrees is about right for all of the outer planets, although Neptune and Pluto often come with a significant hangover phase that can last for a while, sometimes as long as a year. As many astrologers have pointed out, with Pluto the action (such as physically moving out or filing for divorce) may come *after* the transit has ended. If that's the case, then the knock-down-dragged-out power struggle phase of Pluto precedes the final decision, and as the person goes forward from that point the more intense Plutonian energy usually subsides, at least to a significant degree.

Key Transits

Transits to Venus

When the planet most closely associated with love and relationships is transited during a break-up, the partnership itself is of course affected, but so is the person's style of relating in general. New and different styles, patterns, and ideas about relationship are trying to emerge as the present relationship concludes. Look for hard aspects (conjunction, square, or opposition) to Venus.

Transits to the Seventh House (House of Relationships)

This transit usually affects the specific relationship directly, while the person's overall approach to relationship may or may not be undergoing a change. It is probably a good idea for the person to learn to incorporate some of the lessons of the outer planet that is transiting the house, especially if the planet has actually entered the seventh. In addition to ingresses into the house of relationship, look also for squares, although these are more subtle in their effects. An outer planet going over the ascendant will transit the seventh by opposition, and in this case the emphasis is usually on the changes the person needs to bring into their own lives, and relationship is affected by this more basic need.

Transits to the Ruler of the Seventh House

Here, it is often the partner that is undergoing a process of change, and the native can be in a role rather like an observer. The transited planet will often say more about what the partner is experiencing than what the native (assumed to be your client) is undergoing. It can happen that the partner's transit is not necessarily focused on the relationship per se, but the partnership is affected as a result. For example, if Pluto is transiting the ruler of the client's seventh house, it may be that his or her partner is experiencing Plutonian stress at work, and the resultant financial and self-esteem issues are putting pressure on the relationship.

Transits to Planets in the Seventh House

When tenants of the seventh are aspected, we generally get specific information about client's partner. Planets in a house often represent specific people, or a type of person that keeps showing up in that area of the native's life. For example, Pluto in the sixth house may indicate that the person finds a *bitchy coworker* at every job. In the seventh house, we see a kind of archetypal partner that adds an additional dimension to the image of the partner. A woman I know with Jupiter in the seventh has tended towards very large men, just to give a literal example. In terms of the transformative work to be done, we can see that the native who experiences a break-up under this kind of transit is called upon to become fully aware of what that type of person means in his/her life, and to more consciously incorporate the energy—perhaps no longer needing to have that energy expressed by a partner but included in one's own personality. Conjunctions are usually the most powerful. A square may indicate that patience with the partner is growing short, while an opposition may indicate that the partner has some new opportunity or issue to work out.

Transits to the Sun and Moon

Once upon a time, these would have been considered major relationship aspects, because the sun and moon were associated more closely with relationship. The sun in a woman's chart was her husband, the moon in man's chart was his wife. That thinking is pretty much outdated (but not entirely—it persists for some people), but transits to these important planets can indeed correlate with relationship endings.

Transits to the sun can function on two levels, the soul and the ego. On a soul level, significant transits can mean realignment towards one's deeper purpose. If a relationship is not serving those needs, it may need to be released. On an ego level, powerful transits can get us to think too much or too little of ourselves, and thus place pressure on our partnerships.

Transits to the moon can be more challenging, as the moon represents both our comfort zone and our vulnerability. Outer planet transits to the moon thus affect the sense of security. When a hard transit correlates with a break-up, the person often feels abandoned or fearful, although that is not always the case. The lessons of transits to the moon in a break-up almost always center on the person becoming stronger and more independent. The primary lesson is frequently not about relationship in itself, but about reducing the feelings of dependence that we often attach to our partnerships.

Transits to Mars

Unless Mars is in some way associated with another relationship planet, we don't usually think of it in terms of partnership. If Mars is in aspect to Venus, or tenanting or ruling the seventh house, it becomes easier to see how transits to Mars affect relationship. However, sexuality is an important aspect of our partnerships (as I said in the chapter on Mars), and we all know that romantic relationships often end as a result of some kind of tension in the area of sexuality. If this is the primary transit that you see in a client's chart, then it makes sense to inquire about the sexual health of the relationship. Despite progress by leaps and bounds in becoming more open about sex, it is still a sensitive area for many people, so you may need to tread softly.

One other possibility for Mars transits is that anger and motivation are being stirred up in one or both of the partners' charts. For example, a Uranus square to Mars can result in an irritability that can make it hard to stay in a relationship that is not particularly satisfying. Anger and other difficult emotions need not be part of the picture with transits to Mars, however, and what we can see instead is a great motivation for independence, and the courage to break free of a confining situation.

Transits to Saturn

It may be the least likely planet on your list of relationship candidates, and indeed Saturn is more often associated with work and career than relationship. But in a more general way, Saturn represents structure and limitations in our lives, and when it is affected by a powerful transit from one of the outer planets (including sometimes itself), we may be called beyond the boundaries of the way we have defined ourselves. Such a radical restructuring of the sense of self can surely affect our partnerships. For example, consider someone who lives a very buttoned-down, conservative lifestyle, and then finds his or her self in the midst of Neptunian changes that open the world of spirit in a powerful way. They may begin to see that they have been living a life of Saturnian duty rather than truly open hearted love, and so may need to rethink their relationship with their partner.

Cyclical Transits

The transits of the outer planets to themselves in a person's chart are not specifically associated with break-ups, unless the planet rules the seventh or is otherwise associated with the house, or with Venus. Yet these transits, which occur at predictable times in each of our lives, can have an effect of relationship.

The Saturn cycle, which hits a hard aspect about every seven to eight years, is about building structure in our lives, and often correlates with hardline yes-or-no type decisions. A relationship that is under stress at these times may be discarded into the *No* pile. The sobering atmosphere of the first and second Saturn returns is particularly significant in terms of continuing relationships.

Uranus' rebellious energy and the quest for individuality show up during the hard aspects to its natal position, about every 21 years (with some variation, so always be sure to check the actual chart!). Particularly if the person views the partnership as limiting or inhibiting free expression of who they are, the Uranus cycle may coincide with a break-up.

The Neptune square to its natal position occurs around age 42, and together with the Uranus opposition and Saturn's opposition to itself at age 44 is considered one of the *midlife transits*. The

Neptune square closes the door on one's preferred mode of escapism, and can have a daunting effect on one's fantasies about relationship. It is possible to get swept up in a new partnership that one perhaps overvalues, or to be disillusioned with an existing relationship.

The midlife transits, taken together, represent a major change in a person's life, and their partnerships are often involved. While the famed midlife crisis has a bad reputation among those who prefer to hold fast to a stable, Saturnian reality, this time is really an opportunity for renewal and growth. It is somewhat reminiscent of the awkward and tentative transitions of puberty and adolescence, and that is not great for one's ego. Yet failure to make the appropriate transitions is in the end usually far more damaging than the missteps one may make in trying to find a new path in life.

Aspects to the Composite and Other Charts

The above aspects apply to transits to the composite as well as the natal chart, and it may be in the composite that one finds the key to understanding the break-up. In the composite chart, a transit to the ascendant or its ruler, the midheaven, or IC would all be considered as strong as a transit to the descendant/seventh house, and a transit to the sun or moon would be as strong or maybe even stronger than a transit to Venus.

Although I usually use other charts, such as the chart of the first meeting or first date, as background information, it is sometimes possible to see separation stresses in these charts. Occasionally, they hold the primary clue to the relationship ending. For charts based on the inception of the relationship or the chart of a marriage (which is cast for the time that marriage was called for in the invitation), look especially to transits to the sun, moon, Venus, ascendant, midheaven, and chart ruler.

Saturn has a special role in these charts that are based on the beginning of a relationship. The Saturn square at 7 ½ to 8 years is famously associated with the *seven year itch*, and indeed represents a decision point in the relationship, when each partner needs to decide if they will move forward. The Saturn opposition at 14 to 15 years has a similar energy, and one that may even be stronger and require more of a commitment. The closing square around 22 years into the relationship represents another turning point, and there is frequently a feeling of now-or-never if one wants to get out of the relationship. Although it may seem like the Saturn return of a relationship at 29 to 30 years represents a done deal, it is not unheard of for people to see this as an opportunity to leave, often with a feeling of completion of the tasks of the partnership. Especially as we move past the sense of age limitations in our culture, we will see more people ending relationships relatively later in life. Even moving into the second Saturn cycle of the relationship, there may be break-ups at the opening square and beyond.

Uranus is the only other outer planet that can really have a powerful effect by aspects to its position at the beginning of a relationship. It's square to its own position around 21 years into a relationship coincides roughly with the closing Saturn square at 22 years, and may provide additional impetus to leave the partnership.

Aspects

Considering the specific aspects involved often does much to illuminate the process of a break-up. In your interpretations, avoid hard-and-fast rules, but use the following guidelines to inquire about the dynamics of the separation. All of the following refer to an outer planet aspecting some significant planet or point in one of the partners' charts, in the composite chart, or in the chart of a significant date in the relationship.

Conjunctions

Conjunctions are both the ending of one cycle and the beginning of a new one. Although I like to say that the energy of any transit is open and flexible, with conjunctions it really is up for grabs. We may find that the experience can be a complete renovation of the area of life involved, a time of radical change. Yet because one cycle is winding down to a conclusion and the next has not really begun, we may also find that although the person experiences significant internal changes, nothing much happens in an overt way. There can be a vague feeling that something is going on, but nothing takes place immediately. To a great extent, it depends on the nature of the transiting planet— Uranus is more overt than Saturn, for example.

The great lesson of conjunctions is the clearing away of old patterns so that newer and hopefully more healthy and productive ways of relating can be developed. In the context of a separation, the emphasis needs to be on learning from past experiences and developing a sense that past relationship patterns do not need to be repeated. The more awareness the person has about their expectations and needs, the easier it is to evaluate them and decide what should be kept and what should be discarded. In a sense, no matter how much is happening overtly in the person's life, conjunctions should be treated as internal processes as well.

Sometimes, as a relationship ends there is a tendency to begin a new one, a phenomenon we'll discuss within the chapters on each of the outer planets. When a conjunction is the primary aspect in the break-up, it makes sense to be a bit cautious about new relationships—cautious, not discouraging—only because the energy for a new partnership is often lacking until the new cycle is really underway.

Similarly, relationships that begin at the end of a cycle (this is particularly true of Saturn) may not have the energy to go forward past the conjunction. Of course, that isn't always the case (nothing is always the case) but it can be useful to have that in mind when a client is in the midst of a break-up. It is often the case that a relationship that began in the last sextile (Saturn) or semisextile (the other outer planets) of the cycle is really about living out and exhausting the potentials of the old cycle, and there is limited relevance to the emerging cycle.

Squares

In general, squares represent points of internal tension. When a client comes to you in the midst of a break-up and you see a transiting square as the prominent aspect, you know that the tension has reached a point where it has been converted into action. Very likely, it is the partner with the square in his or her chart who has initiated the separation. However, squares do not always function consciously, as they represent two essentially incompatible attitudes and one of these may be repressed. Therefore, it is also possible that the person with the square has in some way withdrawn from or even harmed the relationship in some way without consciously intending to leave. It is then left to their partner to recognize the need for the relationship to end. Now, be careful that you don't jump to any conclusions and wind up accusing a client with a square of sabotaging the relationship so that they can leave. But even if they seem shocked and devastated by the loss of the partnership, probe around gently to see if they don't recognize any potential value in the transition. There is often an upside to break-ups when a square is involved, although it may be hard to recognize.

On a more practical level, you may find that the person with the square has tension between the relationship and some other obligation. Let's say that your client has Venus in the seventh house, being squared by transiting Saturn in the tenth. The issue may not be relevant to the internal dynamics of the relationship at all, but instead be due to career pressure on the partnership. Perhaps the client has to devote so much time to work that there is less attention given to relationship. A classic square scenario would involve a major opportunity for career advancement—but one that would involve moving across the country and thus ending the relationship.

There are two squares in each cycle, an opening square and a closing square. The opening square occurs when the transiting planet is 90 degrees and moving away from the transited planet or point (i.e., the square after a conjunction), while the closing square occurs when the transiting planet is 90 degrees away and moving towards the transited planet (i.e., moving towards conjunction). The difference is subtle, but important enough to be of practical value.

Opening squares are usually more overt, and it is easier to recognize the tensions that are pressing on the relationship. Motivation to move on and start something new may be quite high and obvious, and problems with the status quo are usually stated very explicitly. The opening square is more impulsive, and often more hopeful, than the closing square.

Closing squares come as a time of reflection and assessment. Because we are concerned with break-ups that are in process, we will again assume that the tension is sufficient to result in action, but in general closing squares are less likely to bring about obvious changes. When a separation occurs during a closing square, it is generally with a sense that "enough is enough" and it is time to cut one's losses. It is less hopeful than the opening square, and the emphasis is on getting away from the past rather than moving towards the future.

Oppositions

Always fertile ground for the astrologer's imagination, oppositions often involve projections, and projections usually mean something (or someone) is happening to the partnership. Conjunctions can be deeply internal processes, resetting our relationship clocks for a new cycle. Squares may bring about crushing tension, but will not always be released into action. Oppositions almost always involve an observable event.

The best approach is to simply ask what is happening. If an opposition is already active (the first hit of the transit has occurred) there will usually be a clear answer. If the first hit is approaching, the client may have some idea of what is going on, but may be unsure. For example, if Uranus is approaching an opposition to the client's partner's Venus, the client may have a vague sense that the partner is interested in someone else, but not really be sure about it. You may hear something like, "She says she wants to leave because things are not working out between us, but I think she has feelings for one of her coworkers." The astrological symbolism would suggest that it is a possibility,

74

although the astrologer should be careful not to definitively confirm that it is the case.

If the client has an opposition in his or her own chart, it may be the case that someone new has entered into his/her own life. However, you can't be sure based upon the astrological symbolism alone. Neptune opposite Venus may mean that an idealized new love interest comes into the client's life, but it could also mean that the client's partner fades away in some way or another. That fading away could involve another love interest for the partner, but it could mean many other things, as well.

It is often the perception of the person with a transiting opposition that something has happened to them, that someone has come into or gone out of their lives. However, that is not necessarily either the perception or the reality: it is just as likely that an internal want or need that could not find expression in the past has found a suitable person or situation to project onto. If Ron has been living a quiet suburban life with his wife and kids for 17 years and he suddenly falls in love with someone he meets on a business trip, we *could* say that Pluto crossing his ascendant (opposite the 7th house) brought a new person into his life to transform the status quo. But we should also recognize that there must have been some unmet need or unfulfilled desire that was in a sense waiting for the transit so that it could be expressed. Questions of whether transits originate from within or without are interesting, but like the chicken/egg question they are often unsolvable.

Easy Aspects: Trines and Sextiles

These aspects have a good reputation among astrologers, and may not be immediately associated with relationship endings. However, trines are often considered to be associated with *release*, and it may be the case that the relationship is released under a trine. The easy part is usually that the separation goes relatively smoothly: it may be painful to a degree, but not traumatic; there may be practical matters to attend to, but not long legal battles; and so on. Trines seem to loosen our attachments during their operative periods, and we may find that the relationship is let go of during the trine, but a hard aspect is needed to initiate action. Neptune trine to the moon can ease security issues by increasing a sense of spiritual connection, thus allowing a release that manifests when Saturn squares Venus.

Remember that when we consider partnerships, we are looking at a minimum of two charts, so that one partner can experience the release while the other initiates the change, or that the composite chart may have the tension that ends the relationship while the charts of the two partners contain trines indicating a readiness for release. The closing trine of a cycle, like the closing square, has to do with assessment and letting go of the past, while the opening trine has a more hopeful energy that looks to the immediate future.

Sextiles are not generally strong enough to be the main transits associated with break-ups, although there are exceptions, particularly when they occur after an extended period of more challenging transits. Sextiles are usually associated with *opportunities*, and these have to be recognized and actively engaged in order to manifest. So, a Uranus sextile to Venus may indicate an opportunity to find new relationship options or to leave the current situation, but is unlikely to precipitate a significant change without additional pressures coming from another transit, unless the person is really ready to make a change and has been consciously holding back.

One question that comes up now and again with sextiles is the effect they have on repairing the relationship, as the aspect is often associated with some kind of *support*. It is true that the presence of sextiles during a separation may indicate therapy or some other helpful factor intervening in the process, but that doesn't mean that the break-up does not proceed. Some couples go through a therapy process in order to resolve outstanding issues even though they know they will separate. Others may consult with the clergy or find supportive friends. Pluto sextile to Venus might mean that one finds a really good divorce lawyer or consults a financial advisor prior to initiating legal action (Pluto sextile the ruler of the seventh might mean the partner finds a good lawyer).

The Quincunx

Much has been written about this aspect, but it is not very well understood among astrologers. When aspects were regarded as occurring by sign, rather than degree, planets six signs away from each other were said *not to see each other*, and were labeled as *inconjunct*, a term that also applied to planets in neighboring signs. Planets that are inconjunct do not share the same element, mode, or polarity, and thus have no common basis for communication. Shouldn't be a big deal, right?

Apparently it wasn't, until we began to narrow in and use degrees rather than signs (a product of better ephemerides and a more precise mathematical approach, among other things). Using degrees, we can specify the exact point where the planets are 150 degrees away from each other, and so the quincunx becomes an aspect in its own right. But what does it mean? Vague terms like *adjustment* don't seem to fit very well, or rather they seem to apply equally well to almost any aspect—doesn't a square require that we make an adjustment?

The root of the issue, in my opinion, is that the two planetary energies cannot be resolved into any convenient, compact statement. Each planet symbolizes a type of energy, those energies are moving in unrelated directions, and because they are at the same degree that energy is expressed *simultaneously* (otherwise, it would not be a problem). What we have, then, is two incompatible perspectives expressing themselves at the same time. To the extent that we demand a simple, coherent explanation from the aspect, we are bound to have difficulty because no such explanation is possible—it cannot be resolved even into a this-or-that choice. That is probably why the quincunx in the natal chart is so often associated with health issues: there is lingering psycho-emotional tension that works beneath the surface much of the time because most people have trouble consciously living with psychic discord and inconsistency. *Unconscious* discord is no problem for most, but that can lead to health problems, accidents, and so on. The trick to the quincunx, therefore, is to be able to hold two incompatible perspectives in consciousness at the same time—something that demands rather advanced cognitive and emotional intelligence.

Transiting quincunxes can be quite significant for relationship endings. Although for the purposes of this book I don't really distinguish between the power of the four outer planets, when it comes to this aspect, I will emphasize that farther away the planet and the slower its motion, the greater the effect. That is, transiting Pluto by quincunx is far more significant than transiting Saturn. But we are not predicting separations, we are trying to understand them, so what is the meaning of the quincunx in this context?

As I've already said, the quincunx resists any attempt to simplify it into basic terms. What we usually see is that an area of life that is not particularly related to relationship winds up competing with the energy that would be devoted to partnership. A client with an eleventh house Venus in Virgo had transiting Neptune in Aquarius in the sixth. In this case, there was actually a degree of correspondence, as the sixth house/Virgo energy was present on both sides of the equation. However, with Neptune in the sixth, the client became quite concerned with her work. She was a nurse, and the strain of working in health care, dealing with a decaying system, and seeing so many suffering people on a daily basis was completely incompatible with any kind of romantic feelings for her partner. In Neptunian fashion, she slid into a quicksand of giving all of herself to her work, while her partner cried out for attention.

At first glance, this may seem like a square relationship, a conflict between relationship and work (seventh and tenth houses). Yet with a square, my client would have been far more conscious of the choices she had to make. As it was, she was not really aware that she had made any choice at all—she didn't quite understand what had gone wrong with her partnership. Her issues at work did not seem particularly relevant to her romantic life, and after all it wasn't like she would have to choose one over the other the way she might if her job had asked her to move to another part of the country. Finding and making conscious the effect of the quincunx is challenging for both client and astrologer, but when this aspect is prominent it is worth the attempt.

Minor Aspects

There are as many of these as you like: semi-squares, semi-sextiles, quintiles, septiles, noviles, and more. In my experience, the semi-square will help to shed some light on the conditions of the break-up, but is unlikely to be the main theme. The other aspects may point to subtle stresses (semi-sextiles) or potential opportunities. As you go deeper into a particular narrative—perhaps in the context of ongoing astrological coaching—these may be of considerable use, although for both the astrologer and the client it is usually more helpful to focus on the major aspects.

Progressions

Transits are usually the key when things are happening in someone's life. Even major internal upheavals usually correspond to transits rather than progressions (I am speaking here of secondary progressions, when the chart is moved forward one day for each year). Progressions represent a much more subtle level of change. They indicate a *readiness* to use the energies involved, a *potential* for awareness that is not necessarily activated until a transit aspects one of the planets involved. In a sense, all of our relationships involve working out internal processes with the help of other people. With transits, we tend to recruit others to play specific roles. Progressions tend to be do-it-yourself projects where the assistance of another person is not necessarily needed.

The orb for a progression is much smaller than for a transit, about one degree approaching and separating. Separating orbs are relevant if the progression is likely to be more overt (see below) or if a significant transit is also taking place. Really, though, once a progressed aspect has formed, the awareness that it brings should remain with the person.

79

Only the fastest moving planets by progression (moon, sun, Mercury, Venus, and Mars) can form new aspects, while the others will only perfect an aspect in the natal chart. If Jupiter is two degrees away from an opposition to Pluto in the birth chart, then after a number of years the two planets will either move into a progressed opposition (counting the movement of both planets by progression), or Jupiter will progress to an exact opposition to natal Pluto (actually, both will happen).

Faster moving planets will often move through a few signs during a person's life (the moon moves quite quickly, circling the chart in about 28 years). This means that natal aspects can be modified by progression. Someone with a natal Venus square to Mars can have progressed Venus in trine to natal Mars at some point (probably in their thirties). That opens up the potential to work constructively with the energy of these two planets, seeing their relationship in a new light. Of course, an easy aspect like a sextile can also progress into a square, bringing some tension between two planets that are harmonious in the natal chart. That can have the effect of making the person more conscious of the natal potential, and so can be very productive for the energy of the planets involved. In any case, the natal aspect takes precedence over the progressed aspect in interpretation, but the progression describes how the individual can become more aware of the natal pattern by seeing it in a new light.

Some progressions do tend to be more overt. The conjunction of the progressed sun to Venus (or vice-versa) is one example, and it is directly relevant to relationships and break-ups. The solar principle of *I am* and the Venusian *I love* come into alignment with this aspect. This progressed aspect can form any time up to about age 46 (the maximum elongation of the sun and Venus). When it happens in someone of relationship age, there is an awareness of what love means in the person's life. This is often thought of as a marriage aspect, and indeed people are often ready to marry when this aspect forms, but if someone is in a relationship that is not in accord with their inner experience of love, they may decide to leave the partnership. I have seen people rush into engagements under this progression, only to break it off after a short time. Apparently, this aspect can have the same sort of effect as getting a new driver's license—you are ready to go anywhere with anyone just to try it out.

The progressed semisquare of Venus and the sun is more challenging (people who have a natal semisquare get the progressed version at almost the same time as the progressed conjunction). At this point, the solar and Venusian principles move in different directions, and tensions can emerge. Even when there is great affection and love, the relationship can be seen as thwarting personal expression. On the other hand, it may be that the desire for love and connection overwhelms the person's sense of individuality, and they may give too much for love.

When Venus and Mars form a hard aspect by progression (either progressed-to-natal or progressed-to-progressed), there can also be tensions between asserting one's individuality and cooperating within a relationship. There can also be recognition of issues arising around sexuality and relationship. For example, natal Mars in Aquarius may seek a variety of sexual experiences, while progressed Venus in Scorpio is more concerned with deep emotional connection. This example is obviously similar to the way we would interpret a natal square of these two planets. However, what is unique about the progression is that the aspect is new, and perhaps the first time that Mars and Venus have been in aspect in the person's life.

One final set of progressions to consider is Venus in hard aspect to the outer planets. In this case, if it is not a matter of a natal aspect perfecting, then Venus will progress to the natal outer planet (or the progressed outer planet—it usually is in orb for both at the same time). These aspects can coincide with the changes we will be discussing in the next four chapters, although the flavor of a break-up will generally be colored more by relevant transits. What the progression will cue the astrologer into is the deeper meaning of the time. Note that Venus in progression to the outer planets often manifests at some point after the exact aspect has been made, as inner alignment usually precedes outer changes with progressions.

Incidentally...

It isn't exactly a timing issue, but this seems like a good place to mention house rulers and tenants. When considering the meaning and mechanics of a break-up, it is most important to focus on the outer planet transits to important relationship points. However, the process is often illuminated further by the house rulerships of the planets involved. In fact, we can consider both the natural rulers (e.g., Venus for the second house, via Taurus) and accidental rulers (Venus rules the fourth house in a client's chart if Taurus or Libra is on that house cusp). Further, the transiting and transited planets will both have natal house positions in the client's chart. All of these will throw some light on the dynamics of the break-up, although I cannot stress enough that the big picture is usually more important to the client than the details, however fascinating they are to the astrologer and however much it may impress the client.

For example, a client with Scorpio on the midheaven has Leo on the seventh house cusp, so that Pluto rules the tenth house and the sun rules the seventh. We'll say that natal Pluto is in late Libra in the ninth house, while the sun is in early Cancer in the sixth house (that way they are square by sign but not by degree). By transit, Pluto in Capricorn opposes the sun, and at the same time the client's partner leaves the relationship. The most important point is the Pluto transit to the ruler of the house of relationship, and for all practical purposes we will describe this as a Plutonian break-up. But we can say more, too. First, we would note that it is the sun that is opposed by Pluto, so it is not just relationship but the deeper sense of being and purpose that is being affected—it is a transformation of identity, and relationship is one aspect of that process but not the totality. Pluto rules the midheaven and the sun is in the house of work and service, so we may find that career issues have a part to play in the separation. Perhaps the client has been very busy at work, or it may be that the client's partner has had a change in career status. With natal Pluto in the ninth house, something to do with travel, higher education, religion, or publishing may play into the scenario. Since transiting Pluto is in the twelfth house, we may begin to consider a karmic component, and perhaps something hidden or transformative spiritual experiences. You can generate endless possibilities with only a couple of symbols at your disposal, and the more factors you add in, the more complex things become. Complexity, however, isn't always what the client needs, and this information is often most useful to the astrologer as background.

Location, Location, Location

In the process of creating an astrological understanding of a break-up, separation, or divorce, there is one more thing that you may want to examine, particularly if one or both parties have moved from their birth locale: the locational astrology of each chart. For example, it may be that a natal fifth house Uranus becomes angular on the seventh house cusp when the chart is relocated to the place where the relationship began or where the couple is now living. It could also happen that a couple meets on vacation, and the location for the beginning of the relationship has Venus on the midheaven, while back at home a completely different vibe prevails, and without the added support of the Venusian influence the relationship has a hard time.

A couple that has been together for a long time may move to a place that is stressful to the relationship, but it may also be that the new locale is especially stressful for one partner. For instance, it may happen that the couple moves to a city where Theo has Pluto on the midheaven, and a number of Plutonian experiences take place. This may not seem to be directly relevant to the relationship, but we would have to note that Theo's life is taking on a more Plutonian tone in the new location. On the other hand, if Pluto were on the ascendant in the new location, we would expect a more direct effect on relationship, as this point is opposite the seventh house.

Onward...

Astrology is complex, as you know. In this chapter I have endeavored to offer some basic principles as they apply to relationship endings, but I haven't made any attempt at being comprehensive. Each astrologer has a particular set of techniques and ideas that they apply to chart analysis, and any of these may be valid for examining the end of a relationship. By all means, use midpoints, solar arcs, tertiary progressions, Arabic parts, and whatever else you feel is relevant.

As we go through the next four chapters, we will be dealing with the heart of the matter: the four outer planets and the way they color relationship endings. In this chapter I have given some clues about where to look, with the understanding that there may be many more places. Now it is time to consider what we are looking for, and what it means.

Chapter 7
Uranus

Uranus – The Awakener
Style of Change: Sudden, Unexpected Transitions; Change for it's own sake; Shock!

After 38 years of marriage, Shelley was sure that she knew what her relationship was about. Then one day her husband Don came home with some news: for the past twenty years he had been having an affair with another woman, and he had a fifteen year old son with that woman. He had to tell Shelley because he could no longer keep up his financial obligations to his son in secret. Within six months, Shelley and Don were divorced.

Uranus works like a lightning bolt, shaking a relationship from out of the blue. Even the person who initiates the break-up can be surprised at the speed things happen. One day everything is status quo in the partnership, the next both people are single.

Like Shelley, they don't see *that* coming.

Many relationship endings have an element of shock in them, because we tend to lean on relationship so heavily for our sense of stability. Even when things have been deteriorating for a long time, the final blow that puts an end to a dying relationship can come as a surprise. What you'll see when Uranus is the planet involved is a swift, decisive move on the part of one or both partners.

Just like a thunderstorm—a very Uranian event—you'll see that the initial flash of lightening and clap of thunder is often followed by a series of shocks. Throughout the Uranian period, the attempt to get back to some kind of normal is likely to be thwarted. It's a period of about a year when the desire to find some kind of status quo is probably going to be frustrated. A flexible attitude towards change, often demonstrated when mutable signs are involved, is likely to be a great help. The essence of the Uranian message is not that *this* is better than *that* (although it may be), but that we can make changes, experiment, and remain flexible. More fixed energy can be too concerned with returning to a state of normalcy before it is really time to do so, while cardinal energy has the tendency to move on to something or someone new more quickly, a strategy that risks both failing to process the loss of the partnership and getting into a rebound relationship. With Uranian change, *not knowing*, and accepting that one does not know what is going to happen, is invaluable.

Allison was a mother of two children, living a comfortable suburban life on Long Island. Her husband worked at a good job in the city, and her kids were in high school and junior high, leaving Allison a lot of time for shopping, lunch with her friends, and some community work.

"One day," she recalled, years later, "I was reading the business section of the *Times*, and I said, 'this is me, this is what I am supposed to be doing.' And I left."

A year later, Allison was in graduate school in another state. Her relationship with her husband was over, and those with her children would be severely strained for years to come. A transit of Uranus over her midheaven, uniting both ninth and tenth house

86

energies, coincided with Allison's decision. The almost simultaneous transit of Uranus to her ascendant fueled her decision to make changes in her life. That the seventh house of relationship was also affected was almost an afterthought at the time, and even with lengthy hindsight Allison did not express any regret over the ending of her relationship.

Although her story is a dramatic, it is not all that atypical of Uranian break-ups. The great emphasis that Allison placed on her own needs (transit to the ascendant) and to her career (tenth house) and school (ninth house) superseded any considerations about the partnership. With Uranus, a *me first* attitude often prevails, coupled with a determination to make real changes and make them quickly. Moving away *from* an unsatisfying relationship may be the primary motivation for many people, but moving *towards* a more fulfilling life for themselves is also a strong possibility. Relationship very often takes a back seat in terms of priorities. It may be that leaving the partnership is not the core issue for the person with a Uranus transit, but a kind of side effect of changes they feel they need to make.

Emotionally, Uranian break-ups can be a bit on the chilly side. As Allison's story demonstrates, sentimentality can be at an all-time low and even a mother's care for her children can be put on the back burner. Sometimes, the process of leaving is so swift that neither partner has time to process the loss. That is likely to be exaggerated if the partner is the person who is under the influence of Uranus. If your client is having a watery Neptune transit while her husband is being prodded by Uranus, she is likely to feel bewildered by the sudden changes and coldness of her partner.

The positive side of Uranian coldness is that it can help people to put plans into action. Even when they know it is time to leave a relationship, considerations about the partner's feelings, the way things will appear to friends and family, and so on, can put the brakes on the decision to leave. Uranus doesn't allow much room for sentimentality, and while that can be difficult and even hurtful, it can also be what is needed to get things moving.

Uranian Timing

Uranus has a cycle of 84 years, so the 90-degree divisions fall about every 21 years (give or take a year). That's a pretty long time for a relationship to be in existence, so most of the time we'll be looking at something other than the cycle of Uranus to itself (although 21 years also coincides with ¾ of a Saturn cycle, putting pressure on relationships from two planets around that time).

What is more likely is that one of the partners is at a point in life when transiting Uranus is in hard aspect to its natal position, around 21, 42, or 63 years of age. At these times, the urge for freedom and independence is prominent in the individual, and the constraints of partnership—even one that has been going pretty well—can be felt as a burden. The desire to move on and experiment is often very high at these times. The opposition of Uranus to its natal position at around age 42 is one of the significant midlife transits, along with the Neptune square, Saturn opposition, and in recent years the Pluto square to itself.

These transits are known for disrupting the status quo, and the Uranus opposition is probably the most obvious in its manifestation. If Uranus is in the house of relationship or aspecting its ruler either natally or by transit, a break-up is a possibility. Yet even without any direct connection to the seventh house, the hard aspects of the Uranus cycle can push people out of their comfort zones in any area of life, including partnership.

The most common indicators of a Uranian break-up are hard transits of Uranus to Venus or the ingress of Uranus by transit into the seventh house. A hard aspect of Uranus to the ruler of the seventh can also be significant, although I don't feel that it creates the same degree of pressure, and in fact transits to the ruler of the seventh often indicate that the partner is the one to initiate the change. Similarly, Uranus in hard aspect to the sun or moon could serve to create a desire for change that affects the area of partnership, although perhaps indirectly. Uranus transiting over the ascendant is of course also opposite the house of relationship, and this powerful and potentially revolutionary time can reverberate through a partnership. Unlike Uranus in the seventh, however, the effect on relationship is likely to occur when right around the time of the transit to the ascendant, while a break-up may happen after Uranus has been striding through the seventh house for a while.

Depending on the orb you use, Uranus transits last about a year. It is not uncommon that any action will occur right around the first of three exact hits of transiting Uranus to the natal point. In this, Uranus is unlike the other three outer planets, which often manifest later in the series of three or more direct hits. Uranus is all about reversals, so it may be that a person decides to separate on the first hit, then considers reconciliation on a later aspect (and perhaps another break-up later on). Because of the unsettled energy of the planetary energy of Uranus, trying to predict what is going to happen is usually not the most productive course, and in any event we want to encourage as much self-empowered decision-making as possible for any transit the client is experiencing. The point is to try to keep as many doors open as possible during a Uranus transit to the client's chart (or the transit to their partner's chart). The less everyone assumes they know about what will happen, the better.

Pitfalls

When change for its own sake is combined with a strong urge towards individuality and independence, the very idea of relationship can seem confining. Jumping too quickly from a partnership is one possibility, although as with all the separation styles we can assume that there is some value in leaving. Jumping in to a new relationship, however, is a very real pitfall of Uranian times.

Uranus highlights the value of difference. For many people, relationships are the area of life where they would most like stability as they try to recreate the security they had—or didn't have—when they were growing up. Under the influence of Uranus transits, people become more willing to change the channel on their relationship lives, experimenting with new types of people

89

and new types of relationship. In itself, that is generally a positive experience. The problem is, Uranus can push people to leave relationships on an impulse and then get into a new partnership without much reflection.

Janet was in a relationship with Kerry for almost five years, and they had been living together for about four of those years. As Uranus opposed Kerry's Venus, she suddenly announced that she was leaving Janet for someone else. While Janet was a studious and serious, a Reiki practitioner and expert in holistic nutrition for women, Kerry's new partner was a businesswoman with a very tough exterior and a distinctly materialistic mindset. Janet was hurt that Kerry left, of course, but she was also very surprised by the new partner, who was so very different from her. Within the period of the Uranus transit, Kerry decided that the new partner was not for her after all. She was initially rather cool towards Janet, although she briefly considered reconciliation. By the end of the transit, she was dating someone new, but also more or less maintaining her independence.

The problem is not that Kerry left Janet—it may have been time for that relationship to end anyway. Nor is it that she found someone new and different with whom to have a relationship. Rather, it was the forcefulness with which she jumped out of one partnership and into the other, convinced not that she had found true love, for she wasn't very emotional at this point, but that she had found a much better relationship that would be more fulfilling.

The other Uranian pitfall is the tendency towards coldness. When Kerry left Janet, she did so quickly and without the least bit of regret or consideration for Janet's feelings. When her new relationship did not prove to be as ideal as she thought it would be, she left it quickly, too. During the brief time she considered reconciling with Janet, it was clear that Kerry was considering the possibility as though it were a business deal (something that upset Janet about as much as the initial break-up).

In this example, it was not my client who had the Uranus transit but her partner. She thus received the Uranian energy rather than emitting it. Still, she had to deal with Uranian coldness coming from her partner of five years. It was perhaps more difficult to explain to Janet what Kerry was going through than to bring the chilly nature of Uranus into awareness for someone who is actually having the transit.

When your client is having a Uranus transit, it can be helpful to encourage them to make changes with a consideration of others' feelings. Don't try to stop or slow down their process but do encourage reflection. Terms like "burning bridges" or "slamming the door" can help to make it clear that they may later have some regret about the way that they ended the partnership. If it is the partner who is under the Uranian influence, then it may be harder for your client to understand what has happened: it very often feels like the partner has been taken over by another, somewhat ruder, person.

Easy Transits

The easy transits (trine and sextile) of any planet to a relationship point in the chart can indicate an ability to let go without too much trouble. If the transiting planet is Uranus, it may be that one or both partners are ready to try some new experience. There is usually little resistance to the idea of separation. Possibly, it will be viewed as a trial period apart from each other, and the hesitation to fully move on may be the only real sticking point.

Generally speaking, easy Uranus transits are the most overt among the easy transits of all the outer planets. This is because the transition is not only relatively smooth, but because it is accompanied with a degree of *enthusiasm* that might otherwise be lacking. For better or worse, the Uranian lack of sentimentality is present during easy transits as well as hard ones, and this can both help the process and create some opportunities for regret after the fact. But the regret, if it happens, is usually for failing to get closure and truly grieve the relationship rather than for leaving it.

91

Opportunity Knocks

Uranus can knock us off our feet, but we are just as likely to sprout wings as to hit the ground. As difficult as the experience of any separation can be, Uranian break-ups offer opportunities for change and renewal. Although many people crave stability in the area of relationship, Uranian break-ups allow them to see that their assumptions about partnership do not need to be set in stone. In fact, learning to dial into a new station in the area of relationship is perhaps the greatest gift of this style of separation.

The key is to experiment, to try out new things, from independence and living without a partner to finding oneself with a completely different type of person than one would usually consider for a relationship. I've used the word *experiment* a few times in this chapter, because I consider it to be the key to making the most of Uranian times. Yet we should be clear about what it is to experiment.

Uranian experimentation requires the ability to move fully into a new experience on cognitive and emotional levels, while at the same time keeping a piece of consciousness separate in order to observe and evaluate what is happening. This inner experimenter knows that not all experiments give the desired or expected results, and at some point it may be necessary to scale back, change the variables, or even abandon the entire process. It's tricky to maintain one part of awareness aloof while being swept up in the enthusiasm for someone or something new, but it's necessary if a person is going to make the most of Uranus transits.

In general, in a Uranian break-up people move from one set of relationship expectations and patterns to another. They are sure this new pattern is better and will be more fulfilling. Almost certainly, the newness of the change is enthralling to them. The woman who only dated serious businessmen finds herself with a bad-boy biker. The man who thought domestic stability was what he wanted finds himself out with a new person every night. The woman who thought she needed to be in a steady relationship to be happy found that she could enjoy dating without expectations.

Yet this new set of experiences—as valuable and exciting as they may be—often represent a kind of compensation for past patterns rather than the real *right* pattern. So, it is usually neither the old way of relating nor the new way that really wins the day, but the understanding that there are many ways of relating open to us, and that we can move with flexibility among them.

One client had a chart that consisted almost entirely of planets in water signs, with a strong emphasis on Pisces. She was, predictably, quite sensitive and empathic, with a very emotional approach to life. When she underwent her Uranus opposition around age forty-two, she fell in love with a very Uranian man, an Aquarius sun with almost all of his planets in Air signs. His freedom-loving lifestyle was invigorating and a breath of fresh air for my client, who was used to relationships that could be close to the point of being cloying. This is an example of a complementary relationship, and it had many of the problems that occur with that relationship pattern, especially when the partnership forms under the influence of the three outermost planets.

The man would go off for a few days without letting my client know. He maintained several successful businesses, but ran them from a distance and rather poorly (he succeeded despite himself, so to speak). As the relationship wore on and the Uranus opposition wore off, my client became dissatisfied with his aloof attitude and lack of emotional commitment. It was clear to her that the relationship was not going to work out in the long term. However, she learned a valuable lesson as she recognized that she could have partners who didn't fit into her expectations. Although the Aquarian man was not right for my client, she had discovered that not all of her partners had to have the Earth or Water emphasis she was used to in her relationships. The world of choice and experimentation had opened up to her.

What Uranus is trying to teach us is not that *this way is better than that*, but that we can have flexibility in the area of relationship. We don't have to tune in to the same channel every time we put on the television, we can do a little channel surfing to see what grabs us at this moment. True, our first departure from the usual may begin with great excitement and lead to disappointment (or lasting happiness), or it may be traumatic in the initial stages. But Uranian change is about keeping a flexible approach—finding the one right way to do things is not part of Uranian logic.

Five Things to Do During A Uranian Break-up

Uranus presents a unique challenge in separations, because it tends to coincide with rapid change. Fortunately, our minds tend to work just as quickly, opening up the possibility of bringing awareness to almost any situation. With that in mind, here is a list of things you can suggest to clients under the sway of a Uranian break-up.

1) *Think your feelings.* Uranian times are not necessarily all that emotional, but our minds are working quickly. It may not be possible to feel your way through, but you can think about how you and others might feel as the result of your actions. That can help to get perspective on the unseen emotional side of things.

2) *Experiment.* Recognize that changes are not necessarily permanent, and today's good idea may not work out tomorrow. Keep part of yourself aside to assess whether things are really working, and to explore new options.

3) *Count to 10.* Uranian times demand action, and sitting still is not a good strategy. But impulsiveness can be very strong, and building in a little lag time between idea and action makes good sense.

4) *Do something else.* Uranian break-ups, like any significant separation, can be very unsettling. But one advantage of Uranus is that we can keep moving. There's no need to stew in relationship regrets—so do something that has nothing to do with partnership. Spend some time with yourself. Go out with friends. Take on a new (but modest) project at work. It isn't a matter of

ignoring or repressing feelings, but of taking a break from the intensity of Uranian change.

5) *Notice what has not changed.* As much as things change during Uranian times, some things do indeed stay the same. Your relationship has ended. But maybe your job is settled, or your home is the same, or your friends and family remain there for you. Find the islands of stability in the sea of change and go there when things get too intense.

Chapter 8
Pluto

Pluto—Down to the Bone
Style of Change: Death and Rebirth

Todd and Beth were two very straight-arrow suburbanites, born-again Christians with a new house and plans for a family. Then, on a business trip out of town, Todd met Sandy, who was very unlike the moralistic (and moralizing) Beth. Sandy reminded Todd how much he enjoyed fun—including drinking and sex—things Beth had decided were sinful. Reluctantly at first, because of his new-found religiosity, Todd began an affair with Sandy. He managed a double life, going out of town on business trips monthly, for almost a year. Then, one Wednesday evening between dinner and Bible study class, the phone rang. Beth picked it up and after a few seconds called to Todd.

"It's for you," she said, "someone named Sandy."

We can be glib when talking about deep transformation. We can talk about a caterpillar going into the cocoon and emerging as a butterfly. We use terms like *death and rebirth*, seemingly always putting the emphasis on *rebirth*, as though we could just skate past that pesky *death* part.

When Pluto is involved in the ending of the relationship, there is always a degree of death involved, a kind of loss that is beyond the control of the ego. Things may change slowly or quickly, but they will change deeply.

Plutonian change has a bad reputation, and so far I haven't done much to help its image. Let me start off by correcting that. When a break-up is characterized by Plutonian energy, the process is going to be deep and transformative, but it isn't necessarily difficult. The difficulty comes in when we resist change and have a hard time letting go. The challenge is, we are only ready to let go of so much, and when we are pushed to give up just a little more, the problems can start. Who doesn't have a limit to what they will easily let go of? Who isn't holding on to some aspect of their ego, or some object with which the ego identifies? Isn't it only sane to hold onto our sense of self? Our finances? Our lives? Sooner or later, all but the saints (and maybe a few of them) reach the point of saying "enough is enough" and they start resisting change.

It may not be a bad idea. It may be the healthiest option. But that resistance—and I'm not suggesting people shouldn't resist and defend themselves—is what starts the Plutonian wheels turning.

Plutonian periods are times when we tend to lose control, but that doesn't mean that a person undergoing a Plutonian transit will be under the control of others. It is equally possible that it is their unconscious drives and motivations that are really taking over. Volcanic rage emerging from within can lead to all kind of trouble, manifesting as confrontations with the partner, and, sometimes, the law.

The two emotions most closely associated with Pluto are anger and fear. Anger can reach truly frightening levels, so if it is directed at another person it is only understandable that that person would feel fear. Sometimes, the level of anger is so intense that it actually scares the person who is experiencing it within themselves. Fear is a natural reaction when people find themselves confronted with Plutonian anger, but it is also a product of the understanding that things are changing deeply and forever. Even without a significant anger factor, the depth of Plutonian change can be a bit scary.

Anger can be so strong in Plutonian situations because it really is volcanic. Just as a volcano brings up burning rock from deep within the earth, so Pluto brings up unresolved emotions from the unconscious. So, when a man hears his partner is leaving, it is not just the loss of that relationship that he experiences, but all the unresolved emotional material from past relationships, perhaps going back to his sense that his mother abandoned him or did not give him adequate attention.

Fear is so prominent because there is a sense that control is lost. It may be that a manipulative partner is at the core of the loss of control. It could also be that a long legal battle and the possible financial consequences are at the root of the fear. Sometimes, Plutonian fear is almost an essential kind of fear—it is just there because it feels right to be afraid as the person senses that life is going to change in unpredictable ways.

Plutonian Timing

Pluto transits to the usual relationship points can indicate that a person or relationship is undergoing a Plutonian parting. Pluto transits to the sun and moon can also be significant, as the radical energy of Plutonian change does not stop at prescribed borders, and of course the sun and moon have to do with relationship, anyway.

Pluto's cycle is so long that there isn't much in the way of transits to its own position. Pluto will square its placement at the start of the relationship in anywhere from 35 to 62 years, so it is rarely a helpful indicator. The major Pluto transits to its natal position in a person's chart can be significant, although again it is

98

more of a matter of life changes that include relationship than relationship changes per se.

I have not seen much significance in the minor aspects, such as Pluto semisextile to the position at the beginning of the relationship. In a relationship with a strong Plutonian tone, I believe minor aspects could be significant, although it seems to be the case that a hard major aspect from one of the other planets really sets the tone.

Transits of Pluto are very rare: it would not be out of the question to have a single major hard aspect Pluto transit to Venus throughout one's entire relationship history. Plutonian power aside, the transits are also powerful because they often represent a new energy brought into the relationship picture, something the person may have never experienced before (unlike Saturn, which makes such transits about every seven years). The rarity of Pluto transits also suggests that we take an extra look at the soft aspects—the trine and sextile—to see what role they may be playing.

Another odd facet of Plutonian timing is that the action often happens after the transit is completed. It is not atypical for a relationship to be at a difficult point during a Pluto transit, but not end until afterwards. In those cases, the Plutonian coloring may be a little less intense, although you will usually find it without too much difficulty.

Pitfalls

Ellen, my client, was married to a physician who kept her rather like a prized rare bird. She had a magnificent house in a great neighborhood. She had money to buy whatever she liked. What she couldn't have was any degree of independence or any recognition for her considerable intelligence and education. He was the smart professional in the marriage, and she was to be trophy wife.

Ellen was an intelligent woman in her early thirties. She had Capricorn rising and Saturn in the seventh house. The moon, ruler of the seventh, was conjunct Pluto in Libra, in the eighth house. Her husband was a child psychiatrist with a successful practice in the suburbs north of New York City. He was fifteen years older (half a Saturn cycle) than my client, and as a successful, established, older man fulfilled many of the qualities of Saturn. He had a conjunction of Venus and Pluto in Virgo, in the twelfth house.

Their first date (I was fortunate that Ellen remembered details!) had begun with Capricorn rising and the moon in Scorpio, reinforcing the Saturnian and Plutonian themes. The chart for their marriage had Saturn in the seventh and Mars in Scorpio rising in partile opposition to Saturn and forming a grand cross with Uranus and the sun. Interestingly, the ascendant of the wedding was within a degree of the position of the moon at their first meeting.

Ellen had studied alternative medicine, concentrating particularly on the role of nutrition. Her establishment-oriented husband entirely dismissed everything she said along these lines as unscientific mumbo-jumbo. He ridiculed her mercilessly, and continually pointed out that she knew nothing of medicine or science, areas in which he was of course an expert.

In their personal life, he liked her to be home most of the time, and always seemed to find some reason for her to be at or near their spacious house. He greatly prized her for her beauty, and had no qualms about her spending money on clothes or items for the home—things that would ultimately reflect well on him. However, when they were with friends or at a social gathering, he often acted as though she were his beautiful, but slightly dumb, wife.

Ellen *was* beautiful, but she was anything but dumb. In her estimation, the relationship deteriorated rapidly after the first few years of their marriage, as her husband became harder of personality and more controlling. It seems to me, from the outside, that as she became stronger and more truly herself he felt more and more need to control her. Because they had two children, she was reluctant to leave him until things got very bad.

And things did get very bad. His increasingly controlling and demeaning attitude was amplified during her studies. She soon found out from a friend that although he ridiculed her for her views on the role of nutrition and the potential of alternative healing modalities, he was actually recommending such things to his own patients, representing himself as something of an expert in the area.

A series of unpleasant events happened that led my client to pack her bags and leave at one point. When he begged her to return, promising to be different in the future, she decided to give him another chance. That turned out to be a mistake, for the next time she left the house to go out with friends, he called the police and accused her of abusing and then abandoning her children. Nothing came of the charges, but Ellen got to spend a night in jail and experienced the trauma of being wrongfully accused, both legally and maternally. Her husband made it clear that she hoped she had learned her lesson.

She did learn her lesson, and found a lawyer. Soon thereafter, she began to plan to leave again. However, she began to realize how entirely her husband had controlled her life. For example, she had not had a job since she had been married, so finding employment would be a problem. He had control of the bank accounts and the credit cards were in his name, so he could limit her ability to use their financial resources (she did have access to a modest checking account). While she was grappling with these practical issues, Ellen's husband became all the more controlling. Perhaps sensing that he needed allies, he began to bribe the children with expensive gifts and other indulgences (an attempt that was apparently not very successful, but which caused her some anxiety).

It took some time for Ellen to leave the house, but she managed it. She filed for divorce after a couple of years of inability to get out of this very trying situation (she first consulted me during the period after he had her arrested, and it took almost a year for her to finally leave). Yet things did not end there. He became ill at one point, on a weekend when he had the children. Using his credentials as a physician, he assured her it was serious—he had a bad cold but felt it could really be much more. Playing into his Plutonian hand once more, she came back to the house to tend to him for the day. Seeing him so sick and helpless, she began to doubt herself and reconsider the divorce, which was not yet final. With tears in his eyes, he asked her to remain his wife, to recognize what a good life they had together, how much fun they had in the early days, and the beautiful family they had. Ellen said yes, she thought maybe she should stay after all.

No sooner did he hear this than a remarkable recovery ensued. The husband sat up in bed and began to dictate terms: since she had left the marriage, she must accept that she was at fault. She would discontinue her studies. She would need permission to leave the house for any reason, and would not leave while he was away at work, except on errands... A whole list of demands had apparently been prepared in advance, essentially amounting to an unconditional surrender for my client. Recalling the past few years, especially the arrest, Ellen left for good that evening.

Another year of legal wrangling ensued, but Ellen eventually found a place to live on a more permanent basis, and got a good job. The settlement from the divorce was not unfavorable to her, and she used the funds to obtain a masters degree in counseling psychology.

In this example, we can see various kinds of Plutonian manipulation at work: legal, emotional, and financial. We can also see that although she endured a very difficult time for several years, Ellen emerged stronger and truer to herself than she had ever been. Her determination to pursue a degree in psychology (informed by alternative health) represents a healthy contrast to her husband's view of the psyche as something to be controlled with medication. Because the Pluto transit had passed by the time the divorce case was in court, things went relatively smoothly at that point, although it was not the easiest of all divorce trials, either. It turns out that my client had endured enough in the years before the trial that she had good evidence to present, and her husband was reluctant to have too much come out in public. This was a particularly bad Plutonian break-up, but the outcome was one that ultimately empowering, in a way that only Pluto can empower.

Plutonian pitfalls include all sorts of manipulation and subterfuge. But perhaps the real hallmark of Plutonian pitfalls is *the scorched earth policy*, an approach that seeks to annihilate the other. As emotional material from the distant past is brought up by present circumstances and relived in all its fury, people can confuse past and present. There is a sense that they must win— not simply resolve issues but win—at all costs. The very casting of the former *partner* as *other*, or enemy, is already a step in the direction of the *take no prisoners* approach that is associated with Pluto.

The least little provocation suggests going nuclear, and in the process the aggressor can wind up doing as much harm or more to his or her self as they try to do the ex-partner. That is not unexpected, because in the midst of deep Plutonian change no one person's ego is really in the driver's seat. The stripping away of ego is in fact a large part of what is really happening, and the more entrenched and belligerent the ego becomes, the greater its vulnerability.

In counseling clients in the midst of Plutonian break-ups, both sides of the equation need to be taken into account. On the one hand, we need to try to keep clients away from actively exercising the darker side of Pluto. Helping them to find other ways to vent their rage or to work with emotional material is always an option, and a referral to a good therapist—perhaps one who specializes in experiential therapy—is a possibility. On the other hand, we may need to help clients to protect themselves if it is the partner who is resorting to Plutonian tactics. If the client is being attacked emotionally, legally, or physically, the appropriate defenses have to be put in place. Understanding the situation only helps so much when a person is actively being attacked.

One client asked me to pick a good date for his wife to take a lie-detector test. He suspected her of cheating on him, and wanted her to prove she was innocent. I told him that wasn't something I was comfortable doing and tried to dig a bit deeper into their story. It turned out that this was not the first lie detector test he had demanded she submit to, but the second. The first had failed to incriminate her, but the technician who had done the test suggested to my client that although the test results were negative, *he personally felt* the wife was lying. My client apparently agreed, and so wanted a good day for the retest. You can imagine how little love was left in that relationship, as whatever passion had been there was turned into obsession. This is a rather extreme example of a Plutonian scorched earth approach, but things like this happen with people who we would think of as otherwise normal and well balanced.

Easy Transits

An easy Pluto transit, you say? Indeed, even the softer aspects often have a certain sting when Pluto is concerned, but the trine and sextile can be very helpful transits. At the least, the drawn out legal and emotional wrangling of the hard aspects is usually absent. It is also helpful to keep in mind that because Pluto moves so slowly, the soft aspects take on extra importance, as they may be the only aspect Pluto will make during the relationship.

Pluto transits sometimes manifest after the fact, and that is especially true of the soft aspects. That is, a Pluto trine to Venus may last for a year or more, during which the person contemplates leaving the relationship or has doubts about the partner. Yet the move to leave (or the partner deciding to leave) doesn't occur until after the transit is completed. There is something in soft Pluto transits that suggests that we process deeply during the transit but only manage to act when that processing is complete.

A soft Pluto aspect can also indicate that during the break-up the person has a degree of power. A Pluto sextile may indicate a good divorce lawyer or therapist, for example. A Pluto trine to the ruler of the second house may indicate financial strength during the separation process, alleviating a concern that is often a source of fear for people.

Opportunity Knocks

"I don't care what people think."
"You have to be yourself."
People start saying this sort of thing around age fourteen, but I wouldn't take them too seriously until they've been through a few Pluto transits. Pluto really does strip away layers of assumptions and conventions that we have clothed ourselves in, wittingly or unwittingly. We find ourselves confronted with the bare bones reality of what we really are, and what are our core needs. It can be a painful process, but the end result is solid indeed. No other style of change has such potential for core transformation.

Plutonian break-ups clear out the debris of past relationships from this lifetime and perhaps from previous lifetimes. They bring up pain that was buried, and not only pain from prior partnerships but from every area of life. Parental issues typically come up during Plutonian separations, for example. This bringing up and processing of undigested emotional material is difficult, but when it is over it leaves a person lighter, freer, and more centered. Yes, there may be a scar or two and some grey hairs, but appearances—physical or emotional—matter less than before the experience.

So, the great benefit of Plutonian break-ups is the ability to really be oneself in relationships. Giving up too much for the partner or for the sake of partnership can become a thing of the past, as long as the person maintains a degree of awareness during the break-up. As we clear out difficult emotional patterns of the past, we have the opportunity to relate from the heart, at the soul level. Relationships thus become deeper, while paradoxically they also become less important, in that we no longer feel compulsion to be in a partnership. Genuine relating becomes paramount, while the external form of relationship becomes trivial. The days of thinking that we must have only a particular form of partnership, or a particular kind of partner, are usually over.

Creativity is another opportunity that comes with Plutonian separations. A woman I know majored in music in college, but went into business. During her Plutonian divorce, she joined a band, began writing music, and eventually had her very soulful music played on stage and recorded.

Five Things To Do During a Plutonian Break-up

Control isn't always an option during Plutonian times, but sitting still and passively taking whatever the situation throws at a person is not the best strategy. A balance between letting go into the experience and exerting a certain amount of self-protection is difficult, but it is the key to this style of change.

1) *Process your emotions.* Yes, it is difficult to face all the things that are being thrown at you and thrown up from within you. But this is an opportunity to be clear of these very things. Plutonian times are often likened to vomiting—an unpleasant experience in itself that yields relief. Therapy is not a bad idea in Plutonian times.

2) *Protect yourself.* You may not have much control during the break-up, but that doesn't mean you should give up entirely. Get the legal, financial, and emotional support you need. Even if you lose a round or two, you will be stronger for engaging in the process. On one level, Pluto is something of a game-player, and a little careful gaming is part of Plutonian times.

3) *Create!* Don't believe that Plutonian times are not creative! While Plutonian creations may have rough edges, they go deep to touch the core of what it is to be human.

4) *Move!* Sensible exercise, dance, martial arts, and other movement activities can help to process Plutonian energy. Choose

activities that match the dominant emotion and channel it constructively.

5) *Journal.* Writing down your feelings and experiences can be very helpful during a Plutonian period. Reading how you've been feeling through the experience lets you know how much you've been through (but keep your journal in a safe place!).

Chapter 9

Neptune

Neptune—Opening to Spirit
Style of Change: Dissolution of Boundaries

Neil met Katie at a party and was immediately swept away by her looks, energy, and sense of humor. Their relationship moved quickly, and within a few months they were living together. Katie's history of drug addiction seemed a thing of the past, and she rarely drank much, let alone do anything harder.

After only about a month, though, Neil began to feel something was wrong. At first, cash went missing; next, a few checks were taken out of his checkbook. Katie would also go missing for hours, and her sleepovers at friend's homes became more frequent. He returned home on more than one occasion to find his apartment looking like several people had been having a party. When he questioned Katie, she assured him everything was fine, and he was enthralled enough with her to accept that she was being open with him.

As the situation deteriorated, friends tried to help Neil to see that Katie was again using drugs. Despite the obviousness of the situation, Neil staunchly defended her. He was sure that if showed Katie enough love and was supportive enough, she would come around, stop using drugs, and they would get back to the magical place they had been at the beginning of their relationship. It was only when Katie was arrested that Neil finally began to see the light of day.

Neil's story has many of the elements we typically associate with Neptune: addiction, deception, and the desire to be a savior. Happily, he avoided becoming a martyr and sacrificing his own life to save Katie's, although perhaps only because Katie was headed to jail and/or rehab, Neptunian places of confinement.

Neptune doesn't always bring such drama into our lives. In fact, one can go through a profound Neptunian time without anything happening on the outside to give a clue of the internal storm one is experiencing—unrequited love or loving from afar are classic Neptune signatures.

However it plays out, we wake up from the Neptunian dream or nightmare and wonder, "What was *that* about?"

Among the outer planets that we are discussing as break-up styles in this book, Neptune is the hardest to say anything definite about. The subtle energy of Neptune is not easily quantified or qualitatively described, and so we often say that what happens in these times is not what it seems. The lack of clarity and focus and the inability to grasp hard facts can lead to fantasy or delusion, to idealization or demonization, to spiritual enlightenment or paranoia. We can sense that something greater and more powerful is at work, but when we try to pin down that force we find it elusive. If we try to connect it with another person, we usually find that they represent a very imperfect version of the ideal we think we see.

Neptune is so difficult to define because it operates beyond the realm of definition. Neptune is not about *this* or *that*, but rather it calls us beyond the duality of separate things into a spiritual place of *both this and that*, a place where what we see as paradox with our normal consciousness becomes a greater whole with elevated perspective.

Needless to say, this can be difficult where relationship is concerned, what with its real people and their very human capabilities and limitations.

Perhaps the most certain thing we can say about Neptunian break-ups is that a person will have a rather intense experience. But even that is subject to qualification, as the lingering loss of a partner can occur in such a way that one is not fully aware of how much life has changed. Gradually drawn into the movie of the separation, it is possible to accept the extraordinary emotional ups and downs as normal.

Deception is often considered to be the hallmark of Neptune. While Mercury is known as *the trickster*, Neptune is often associated with *the con artist*. Yet it would be unrealistic and unfair to think that one of the partners is somehow deceiving the other during a Neptunian break-up. It *could* go that way, as we have seen in the story of Neil and Katie, or if one of the partners is seeing someone else. Often, though, what people are inclined to think is deception is actually a result of extraordinary expectations not mapping very well onto reality. That things are not what they seem (or what we want) does not mean that active deception is taking place. Bob imagines that Mary is a certain way, and if Mary turns out to be otherwise it is not a matter of her deceiving him. In a sense, Bob deceived himself.

The *victim-and-savior* motif is sometimes present, as we saw with Neil and Katie. When this is prominent, it can lead to one partner doing everything possible to help the other—often with limited positive results for either of them. Addictions come into play frequently in these scenarios, but there is a range of possibilities. Astrologers will be quick to look to Neptunian themes like *places of confinement*, and note that one partner may be trying to rehabilitate someone who has been in jail or a rehabilitation facility, or even an extended stay in a conventional hospital for a physical illness. Indeed, these specific scenarios do emerge, but there are many other possibilities, as well (of course, partnership with someone who has been in jail, etc., does not necessarily imply a hopeless Neptunian experience). One powerful—but less dramatic—possibility that is often seen is that the partner loses his or her job and becomes financially dependent in such a way that it puts a drain on the relationship.

The Neptunian process offers us a way beyond our ego reality, and to do that the boundaries of ego that we live within need to be loosened or dissolved. That alone is a potentially frightening or painful process, but when applied to relationship—the area in which so many of us strive to find security—it can be very intense. Neptunian separations can truly dissolve not only the relationship, but also the ego of one or both partners. Whether that means opening to a higher spiritual reality or simply giving up on life (or love) is the question.

Neptune often plays with what I call our *guiding myth*. A guiding myth is a story we tell ourselves, and an ideal we latch onto. Today, guiding myths often involve idols from the media, whether real people like movie stars and musicians or characters from movies or television. Most of us have several guiding myths, although one may stand out as especially strong. If you love to cook and fancy yourself hosting your own cooking show while making dinner, you have a guiding myth. Far from being idle fantasy, guiding myths can have powerful effects on our lives. The Beatles have stated that they wanted to be as successful as Elvis Presley—something that may have seemed outrageous for a local rock band from the suburbs of Liverpool—and their adherence to their myth had great effect. There is some good evidence that the process of imitation, when combined with determination, does help us to tune into our goals. It is as though we use the myth to guide us into a kind of gravitational field around who or what we want to become. Having some deep internal resonance with the guiding myth helps us to make an ideal into a reality.

111

When experiencing a Neptunian break-up, it can happen that the guiding myth around the area of relationship changes. One way that this can happen is the introduction of a new myth, as when a new person comes in and seems to offer the possibility of perfect eternal love. At such times, there may be a resonance with classic romance stories and contemporary love songs. It can be very hard not to buy into the myth of total and complete love, and in fact it does not make much sense to avoid taking the ride that being in love offers. Yet Neptune often offers more than he delivers, and it could scarcely be otherwise given the idealized image of the partner and the relationship he presents. Neptune may offer the new guiding myth and then take it away all within a single transit of a couple of years.

Another way that Neptune can play with the guiding myth is to take away an existing myth. For instance, a man or woman that has established the myth of the happy, sedate, suburban couple (complete with minivan and kids) may find that that image is no longer energizing. The American sitcom family imagery begins to become more of a burden than a satisfying way of life. The guiding myth is crumbling, and until a new one comes and takes its place, the person may feel that they are drifting at sea.

Whether it is the loss of an existing guiding myth or the gain (and possibly subsequent loss) of a new one, a big part of a person's self image is changing. A loss of a guiding myth is the loss of *who you are*, or *who you were going to be*. Self-image, an important ego function, is changed orlost.

Guiding myths, con artists, tricksters. All of these suggest that the real content of Neptunian times is archetypal in nature, and what people experience is not confined to their individual stories but also includes a deeper dimension of the human psyche. If only we experienced these transits from an objective position, watching the flow of human history with dispassionate understanding! But experiencing the archetypes in all their passion is part of the process, and we don't sit by passively.

Neptunian Timing

Astrologers will probably recognize a bit of irony in the very idea of Neptunian timing, given that the planet is so well known for fogging out or sense of time, among many other things. That is exaggerated with the years-long transit of Neptune, and also with the tendency of Neptune to work subtly. Unlike the other outer planets, a two-year transit of Neptune that affects relationship may not come with any obvious event, external or internal, at the first or even second exact hit.

Still, transits to Venus, the seventh house, etc., can give a rough time frame for Neptunian change. Don't forget to include the Neptune square to its natal position that occurs around age 42. How much that has to do with relationship is an open question, but someone experiencing a break-up at that time is very likely to feel like it is a Neptunian experience.

Although the moon and sun are always important considerations in a break-up, if only to give background information, they take on more direct relevance where Neptune is concerned. Transits of Neptune to either planet can sometimes coincide with and be the major transit of a separation. If a client's transiting Saturn is in an opening square to Venus while Neptune is opposite the moon, you can probably assume that the *mechanics* of the break-up are Saturnian, but your client's *experience* is very likely to be more in tune with Neptune.

Pitfalls

Give until it hurts, they say, and with Neptune that is sometimes just the beginning. Because of the vague energy of Neptune, it is difficult to be specific about the pitfalls that people can fall into during a break-up. However, it is generally true that Neptunian extremes are in evidence.

One extreme is that of loss. We all hurt during a separation, but Neptune can make it seem as though the pain is all there is. To an extent, a person going through a Neptunian separation can be enveloped in pain, and sadness and loss can become their entire universe. It is usually difficult to work with this, because the pain is—in its own way—a kind a drug. There can be something attractive about intense emotional pain, and the surrender to it. Often, people who are going through this kind of process don't want to feel better, they want to go deeper into their own suffering.

That can be difficult to understand from the outside, but there are two sides to it. One dimension is that the pain indicates that there was meaning to the relationship, and if the relationship has given meaning to their lives then people won't want to lose that. The other dimension is that Neptune is ultimately calling us beyond our ego, and in surrendering to the hopelessness of intense emotional pain, we let at least part of our ego die. These two reasons for going deeper into the pain aren't exclusive of each other, and in fact they go hand in hand much of the time. The problem is that without awareness that *spiritual surrender* is what is called for, some people will allow their lives to derail and sink into an abyss of hopelessness. The ego doesn't die to a higher self, it simply continues to stumble around, bruised and confused.

Not everyone wants to sink to the depths of hopelessness and pain, however, and that brings up the next Neptunian pitfall, escapism. A healthy degree of escapism is fine, but Neptunian times can push people very far into alcohol, drugs, and other forms of escape. Even meditation and spiritual pursuits—on one level perhaps the very goal of the Neptunian process—can be taken to extremes, as when a person spends so much time meditating that they forget to pay their electric bill. With Neptune prominent in a break-up, the reality of the situation may be avoided for a long time. That's one of the reasons that with this style of separation we often wonder why the client hasn't already left a dead end situation. After the break-up, it may take a very long time before the client moves on with their relationship life. In both scenarios, there can be a tendency to hang on that is not so much stubborn and fixed in quality as indecisive and mutable.

Don't be surprised if people with a lot of cardinal energy try to escape by moving on too fast. Set adrift in the fog, the cardinal personality will start to row in any direction, chasing the faintest whisper of a bell or an apparent shape looming in the dark mist. The resulting rebound relationship could be very disappointing for the person, as Neptune helps to make even dim possibilities seem like golden opportunities.

One significant pitfall of Neptunian separations is not found in the loss column, but in the potential gains column. People are often called away from their current relationship with the promise of something much better, only to find that the person they have fallen in love with has the same set of human foibles as the rest of us. A client with a stellium in late Aquarius left her husband for a coworker who she saw as far more dynamic, intellectual, and social, only to find that he was also noncommittal and emotionally distant.

Perhaps the most significant pitfall of Neptunian separations is the tendency to idealize or demonize the partner (or be idealized or demonized by the partner). The new partner is seen as a knight in shining armor, or as the black knight that embodies all evil. Because Neptune transits last a long time, people may get into the relationship thinking they have found their knight or princess, only to decide that they have actually hooked up with a dragon. The astrologer should keep in mind—especially when only getting one side of the story—that Neptune transits often correspond with projections of archetypal images, and the wonderful/terrible partner is, in all likelihood, just a person after all. Deflating some of the projection is a worthy goal, although it must be done with some care, as feelings will be intense and raw when Neptune is involved. While Uranian times can also set up ideal images that are enthusiastically embraced, the emotional commitment is usually far greater during Neptunian transits, and thus the potential pain is also greater.

Easy Transits

Easy Neptunian transits often go unnoticed, and frequently no overt event is associated with them. However, if a break-up is occurring and you see easy Neptunian transits in the mix, it is worth considering how this may affect the partner having the transit.

Neptune represents, among other things, our escape hatch, the way we psychologically and physically extract ourselves from difficult situations. When easy transits of Neptune are present during a break-up, there is usually some means of escape offered. Sometimes, it may be that a new love interest is available, although it may not be obvious to the partner. It may also be that some other area of life is getting very energized, so that the person may find that although the relationship is lost they *fall in love* with their job or their new home.

As with any Neptune transit, an ideal is presented and an ideal is lost: the guiding myth changes. With the softer transits, the changes are made more easily and often more subtly. It can be that the loss of the relationship does not make as much of an impression because the person simply glides from one way of being to another without much stress. However, if difficult transits are also present, we can expect that an easy Neptune transit will provide a means of escape and retreat at most.

Opportunity Knocks

The difficulty in talking about the benefits of Neptunian break-ups is not because they don't exist, but because Neptune functions in such a different way than the other styles of change we are discussing in this book. There is usually very little that the ego takes away from a powerful Neptunian experience, and to the extent that we think in terms of the ego (which we all often do), it can seem as though there is no real benefit to the break-up process. Many Neptune transits manifest on levels where almost all we take away is the experience, but the experience of a break-up is rarely considered a benefit. However, if we back up a bit and reflect on it, we can see that there are some opportunities embedded within the break-up experience.

One potential benefit is that people often feel less pressured around the area of relationship after a Neptunian separation. While a truly nonchalant, noncommittal, take-it-or-leave-it approach may not be desirable, a less extreme version in which the person is ready to allow partnership potentials to arise and unfold on their own schedule can be a blessing. Relationship often just doesn't seem to be quite such a big deal after a Neptunian break-up, and priorities can open up into other areas, such as spirituality.

If you listen to popular music (any era in the past hundred years or so), it should come as no surprise that Neptunian separations can inspire creative works. Certainly music, but also books, movies, and other art forms are often Neptunian-themed. While the world may not need another maudlin hymn to lost love, there is no doubt that Neptunian times often translate into creative potentials. The depth of Plutonian changes often inspire soul-level art, and the iconoclastic energy of Uranian times can lead to brilliant insights, but Neptune plays the heart strings very effectively.

Yet ultimately the real value of Neptunian break-ups is to allow us to glimpse something beyond the ego's vision of the world and how it should be. Neptune invites us to experience *what is* on all levels. Neptunian travels to other dimensions of reality can lead some people to essentially check out of everyday reality, and that is of course a problem, but with mindfulness and compassion (towards oneself, especially) it is possible balance the call of the material and spiritual realms.

Five Things To Do During a Neptunian Break-up

Doing something is almost inimical to the nature of Neptune. After all, where would you paddle to if you can't see a destination, and why put an oar in the water if you are being pulled along by an overpowering tide? Yet there are some suggestions for making one's way through a Neptunian separation.

1) *Meditate.* Or pray. Neptune connects us to alternative realities, and it helps to make some effort to try to make those *higher* realities. Trust that your soul is going on the journey it needs for its evolution, and if you can keep a loving, compassionate perspective, so much the better.

2) *Stay sober.* Most of the time, anyway. Neptunian break-ups can really hurt, and drugs and alcohol can offer temporary escapes. There's nothing wrong with a couple of glasses of wine every now and then, but the escape from the pain is only temporary.

3) *Cry it out.* Neptunian separations are watery times, and your own personal waterworks can help you to process your emotions. This is no time for a stiff upper lip, so grab some tissues and wail. A really sad movie can help to get the tears flowing, if needed.

4) *Create!* The openings that Neptune creates in our egos allows for feelings and ideas to come rushing forth. Getting lost in the creative process is perhaps the best escape from the sadness of Neptunian loss, because it also processes the pain.

5) *Ground yourself.* Neptunian times can make us feel disoriented and lost. Unlike Uranian changes, however, we often feel fear and loss rather than anxiety and thrills when we lose touch with the ground. So drop anchor every once in a while. Exercise. Eat a reasonable but filling meal. Do something very earthy, like working in a garden or cooking.

A Reflection for Neptunian Times

Imagine a house with sunlight streaming in through the windows. Some rooms are well lit, facing south, while some are a bit less illuminated. The light comes through the kitchen window, bringing a sunny cheer as the family prepares their meal. Sunlight also reaches into the bedroom, casting a warm glow over the activities that take place there. The large picture window in the living room lets in the sun to brighten meetings with friends. The library is illuminated by sunlight dancing on shelves of books.

How silly would it be to think that it was a different sun that lit each room? How foolish would we think someone who saw the light in the kitchen as being fundamentally different from the light in the bedroom? How crazy would we think a neighbor who believed that the light illuminating their house came from a different sun than the light illuminating ours?

Yet this is what we do with love. We break it into pieces and compartmentalize it. The love between parent and child, between lovers, or between friends are all seen as fundamentally different, as though they not only found different places to manifest in our lives, but also came from different sources. We also make love into a thing to be possessed, as though we could hold onto a beam of sunlight. We can feel jealousy or envy, as though our neighbor somehow has more of the sun than we do.

Certainly, love does find a myriad of ways to manifest, and we don't want to confuse the relationships we have while incarnate. But just as we may appreciate the way the sunlight plays through the living room and also the way it warms the bedroom without thinking that the source is two different suns, we can realize that the love we find in our many relationships is the same love, expressed in different ways.

Our project is ultimately to replace the brick and wood and plaster of the roof and walls of the home with glass, so that light can shine in everywhere. Even when we accomplish this great task, there will still be various rooms and we will meet different people in each of them, but we will be able to recognize all the more clearly that our home on this plane is illuminated by one light—love. Neptunian times are ideal for dissolving the hard opaque structures in our lives, the brick and mortar of Saturnian reality, and replacing it with transparency that lets light shine in all its radiance. For each bit of solid matter that we lose, we open up to more soulful, warming sunlight.

Chapter 10
Saturn

Saturn—When the Bill Comes Due
Style of Change: Difficult decisions, a feeling of necessity

After twelve years of marriage and nearly fifteen years together, Sally and Andy decided to call it quits. They both agreed that whatever they had once had was long gone and now they were just going through the motions. Neither of them was seeing anyone else, and neither really had any enthusiasm to begin something new. When Andy left for the last time, Sally closed the door before he was out of site. Her only real thought was, "Why don't I feel sadder than I do?"

Saturn weighs heavily on us much of the time. When a break-up is Saturnian, it often has a dry, matter of fact quality about it. A decision is made, and that's that. People often recognize that a relationship is beyond the point where it can be healed, and they have a reserved acceptance.

When asked about it, they may respond with a Saturnian, "It is what it is."

Saturn often works through formal channels. The intensity of the other styles of change may be lacking when the ringed planet is involved, and for many couples the Saturnian question is about that most formal relationship, marriage.

For married couples, a break-up could mean divorce, although a protracted period of trial separation—perhaps a never-ending condition—is also a possibility. For couples that are not married, a transit of Saturn could mean that the deadline is reached and a now-or-never ultimatum about marriage is delivered. Regardless of the specifics, it is generally the case the Saturnian break-ups revolve around the *form* of the relationship, if not the formalities. Sometimes, it isn't a matter of marriage, as when one person wants to move to the next step in the relationship (maybe moving in together) and the other hesitates.

One client decided to remain in the marriage with her husband, and they continued to live in the same house and put on the appearance of a family unit, all for the benefit of their children (who seemed none the better for the skewed realities of life within the home and in the community). As Saturn is often associated with delays and restrictions, scenarios such as this are not too uncommon, as it can be difficult to leave the situation in the face of delays. Another client wanted to proceed with a divorce but her husband lost his job and they needed to continue living together despite their mutual willingness to end the marriage.

Age differences that seemed to make no difference at the beginning of the relationship can become more significant as time goes on. When we speak about age differences in astrological (or at least Saturnian) terms, we are generally speaking of seven or more years difference, which is of course one quarter of a Saturn cycle. It is often during a hard Saturn transit that these manifest and lead to a separation—for example Saturn going into or opposite the seventh house or the Saturn return of one partner (usually that would be the first return for the younger partner and the second for the older partner).

Saturnian endings often come with a dulled sense of emotion. Unlike the passionate throes of Pluto, the wild excitement of

Uranus, or the agonies and ecstasies of Neptune, Saturn often indicates an almost blank emotional condition. It is not so much a matter of *sadness* as *depression*. If emotionality is lacking in Uranian break-ups, it is because enthusiasm (or anxiety) is running too high to reflect on the past and what is lost. Neptunian sadness is intense, but active. Saturnian depression is cold, dry, and passive.

Saturnian Timing

Round up the usual suspects: hard Saturn transits to Venus, the seventh house, etc. With Saturn, however, we have an additional timing tool, the cycle of Saturn to its own position at the start of the relationship. Many partnerships break up at the 90 degree marks of the cycle; that is, the opening square at 7 ½ years, the opposition between 14 and 15 years, the closing square at 21 to 22 years, and at the closing of the cycle at 29 to 30 years. Yes, it does happen that couples that have been together for a complete Saturn cycle decide to separate after 30 years, especially in today's world of no age limits.

The famed seven-year itch is the opening square of the Saturn cycle, and with many couples finding this a stressful time, it often corresponds with a decision to take the relationship deeper or to separate. This may be the point at which one partner decides that it is time to get married after years of living together, or that it is time to move in after a long period of more casual relationship.

For marriages, it is quite often the opposition at 14 to 15 years that corresponds to divorce, but we have to be a bit careful about the timing. Saturn tends to work on formal partnerships, and so marriages can come under stress (of course, any partnership that has existed for 14 years has *some* degree of formality associated with it). However, it is usually helpful to time the break-up from the start of the *relationship* rather than the *marriage*. That is, we may see that a couple has been married for 10 years, but has been together for 14 years when they separate. Saturn has an effect on the formal relationship, marriage, but at the 14-year mark *of the partnership*. The same logic applies to timing Saturn at the opening and closing squares of a relationship. My guess is that this is due to the fact that we now tend to have longer times before marriage (including lengthy engagements), and a couple may be together several years before deciding to marry.

The closing square around 22 years and the Saturn return near 30 years are relatively new break-up points. As we remove assumptions about age and vitality, we begin to feel that a new and better relationship—or simply the end of an old and decrepit relationship—is a real possibility later in life. Since the 1970s, the age of first marriage has been getting later, but certainly people that were married before 30 would be under the age of 60 at the Saturn return of the marriage. Yet people in their sixties, seventies, and beyond are coming to understand themselves as intellectually, emotionally, and sexually attractive well past the limits that were perceived only a few decades ago.

One more consideration may be relevant to the timing of break-ups. Saturn, being a very practical planet, can sometimes precipitate change that the other outer planets initiate. For example, one woman with a great deal of Scorpionic/Plutonian energy in her relationships experienced a break-up as Neptune aspected her Scorpio Venus from the later degrees of Aquarius (an opening square). She fell in love with another man, one whom she saw as far more dynamic and noble than her partner and husband of twenty years. However, for various reasons—most of them Neptunian—she kept the new relationship to herself and did not act on it until the closing Saturn square of the relationship with her husband. Thus, Saturn can help to make real the potential of the other outer planets.

In general, Uranus needs no help to get things moving, but there are times when Saturn helps to resolve an internal conflict. Someone with a lot of fixed energy around relationships, for example, may resist change during a Uranus transit. One client had several affairs during a Uranian period, but did not make a move to leave her marriage. It was only when Saturn went over he Libra ascendant that the marriage ended, when she was caught by a private investigator her husband had hired.

Neptunian break-ups can linger for years if one or both partners cannot let go of the relationship. A little help from Saturn can help to consolidate the vague Neptunian energy and lead to a decision. Plutonian break-ups rarely need such help, but the energy of a Saturn transit can put a cap on protracted legal or emotional processes that delay the final end of the partnership.

If one of the other outer planets is prominent in the break-up, then that planet will probably describe the dynamic and feel of the separation most accurately. It will be the planet that needs to be worked with in helping the client to deal with and make the most of the separation. In those cases, Saturn is usually more involved in the timing of concrete steps in the break-up process rather than setting the tone, although clients will also often report at least a little of the Saturnian drag as the transit reaches an exact hit.

Pitfalls

You've made wrong decisions, right?

We all have, and sometimes the consequences are problematic. But when Saturnian times prevail, the worst decision is not to make any decision at all. At the end of the day, not choosing is a choice in itself, and Saturn helps us to understand that it isn't a good one. The prime pitfall of a Saturnian separation is the same as any other Saturnian time: people sit on the fence until it collapses from under them. Clients need to be encouraged to make a decision about the relationship, about moving on or staying and working on it.

It's generally not easy to ignore Saturnian times, of course. The ringed planet is great for focusing our attention on practical issues, and we rarely fail to recognize that there is something that needs our work and care. But at the same time, we often don't feel great about dealing with Saturn's issues—they manage to be just the kind of thing we'd rather wait until next week or next year to really delve into, and if they were to resolve themselves in the meantime, that would be great. As these two impulses—deal with it or procrastinate—compete with each other, time marches on.

Fortunately, a proactive, realistic approach isn't too hard to foster. Saturn often responds to logic and the cold dry facts, and while the tendency to avoid difficulties may be strong, the ability to escape them in a whirl of fantasy is usually absent. When Saturn is affecting a relationship, it is a bit like that noise coming from under the hood of the car—you can't help but hear it, no matter how high you turn up the radio. Key questions might be, "what do you think you can realistically expect to happen at this point?" or "what is the bottom line for you at this point?" That kind of direct questioning can help clients to recognize their options (if indeed there are any) without specifically telling them what the astrologer thinks the situation is or what the client should do.

A second pitfall of Saturn deserves mention, and it is just as prevalent and serious as the first. It is the tendency to believe that the relationship life is over, that the loss of this relationship is the end of all intimate relationships. Saturn is the celestial timekeeper, and under his influence people often feel as though they are getting old and hence they are less desirable. But Saturnian times can also correspond to a general feeling of being unlovable and unworthy of love. It is also a possibility that the person may not feel unlovable, but they feel that they are not likely to love anyone else again. It is an exaggeration, but one that can have a debilitating effect.

Saturnian break-ups are not likely to result in a rapid rebound relationship, although people with strong cardinal energy may be an exception. Rather, after the break-up there is often a down time in relationships that lasts for at least the length of the transit. While Saturn moves fast enough that this usually won't be a very long period of time in the chronological sense, it is often a period of relative depression. Once again, the best strategy is to be realistic. Challenge the client's belief that they could never be attractive to someone else, or that they would never have feelings towards other people again. Usually, Saturnian seriousness cannot escape the cold hard fact that life may very well get better at some point.

Easy Transits

With Saturn, easy is a relative term. When trines and sextiles are present, it may be that there is a general agreement between the two partners that the relationship is over. A practical matter, such as finances or a work issue, is often the focus of the break-up, rather than the partnership itself.

For example, it may be that the relationship has been bouncing along without much in the way of growth—or stress—for some time when one of the partners is offered a new job in another city. The other partner has no intention of leaving their job, and so the question becomes which is stronger, the relationship or career? Such a pivot point may become an unexpected fulcrum in the partnership, raising questions that might have otherwise gone unasked.

Remember that trines and sextiles (or any other aspect) do not mean that a relationship will end—they help us to understand the dynamic of the separation rather than predicting it. That is certainly true with Saturn, where the element of choice is almost always present (if not pleasant).

Opportunity Knocks

We don't usually associate Saturn with opportunities, and within the context of the end of a relationship it may seem like a stretch to even consider that there is an up side. Yet as much as astrologers are inclined to see Saturn as a drag, we also recognize that it helps us to build structure within our lives. Within the context of relationship endings, Saturn can help people to make difficult decisions and to leave unsatisfactory partnerships. It can also help to remove the unrealistic expectations that so often contaminate our relationship patterns.

The decision to leave a relationship is naturally a weighty one. During the process, one partner will consider their own needs, but will usually take into account the partner's feelings as well. Lunar security needs can attach themselves to relationships very easily, as I've already said. Fixed energy approaches to relationships tend to seek stability in this area of life, perhaps using it as a base for adventures in career or other areas. On balance, it can be a very difficult decision to leave a partnership, even when one is not truly satisfied with it.

Saturn rarely makes decisions easy. In fact, Saturn is the champion of setting up situations that appear to be zero-sum choices: no matter what you choose, you gain something and lose something. One of the dangers of Saturnian situations in general is to procrastinate in making a decision, trying to balance between the frying pan and the fire. Yet Saturn often puts enough pressure on us that we eventually realize we have to do *something*. During Saturnian times, we are usually all too ready to avoid making a decision or even thinking about the issue at hand, but we are constantly reminded of it in one way or another. Sooner or later, unless we are determined to make no choice (which is a choice in itself), we have to decide what to do.

Of course, it is also possible that Saturnian changes to relationship originate—or at least seem to originate—from the partner. If Saturn is aspecting your client's Venus, it may be that it is their partner that has decided to leave and your client has no choice to make at all. If that is how things appear to be working out, it is important to emphasize that although the choice to end the relationship has been made by the partner, there are still other decisions to be made by the client. These usually revolve around the emotional response to the break-up. This can be empowering if it is done with awareness, and a proactive approach can help to minimize the danger of the client falling into a state of emotional helplessness, where they feel that there is nothing they can do.

With Saturn, that can mean that a stiff upper lip sort of approach prevails, but that isn't necessarily the attitude that has the most potential for growth because it cuts off the emotions rather than bringing them into awareness and processing them. The ability to recognize what is (or isn't) being felt and then come to a place of acceptance is a far more healing way to work with Saturn. Openly feeling whatever level of grief is or isn't there and accepting it is a start, but from that point the client is challenged to live with the sadness without making it the focal point of their life. If they can realistically assess how the break-up feels to them, and not make the mistake of thinking that their relationship life is over, then clients can come away from the experience feeling empowered rather than abandoned. If nothing else, Saturn is realistic, and usually only a modest amount of coaching is needed to help clients get a realistic assessment of the situation.

Ultimately, the gift of a Saturnian break-up is the potential to see relationship within a more realistic context. Yes, it can be difficult to be wildly romantic afterwards, but with a little awareness and maybe a bit of guidance it is possible to approach future relationships with a firmer sense of what we want and need from a partner, and how much we are willing to compromise (and risk) to get it. All of the separation styles offer the potential to see relationship differently—they may let some air out of the sails but they offer a new perspective. With Saturn, that perspective is about the ability to make realistic choices and contain (not cut off) the emotional fallout from those decisions. Ultimately, that leads to a more solid, more mature foundation for future partnerships.

Five Things To Do During a Saturnian Break-up

On the one hand, Saturn gives us something we have to deal with, something that requires our attention. On the other hand, we also have to contend with delays and tests. Once we decide to dive in and make some changes, we often find that it is not smooth sailing. Here are some suggestions for clients who are in the midst of Saturnian separations.

1) *Deal with it.* You probably don't want to do whatever it is that needs to be done. You don't want to hire a divorce lawyer. You don't want to have *that talk* with your partner. You don't want to start packing, and you don't want to call the phone company to shut off the line. But do it. The longer you delay, the worse you will feel. With Saturn, delay does not lessen pain, it only postpones it.

2) *Be realistic.* Saturn seems to encourage realism, but in fact it can paint a rather pessimistic picture of things. If Saturn were an artist, he would paint only in shades of grey. We thus tend to think that our reality itself is grey. But actually it is only one version of things—just as your neighborhood on a grey November day is only one reality, and a sunny May afternoon is just as real. Time pressures, the sense that your relationship life is over or that you will never love or be loved again are not realistic. Think it out.

3) *Patience.* Even when you decide you will face the realities of the break-up head on, Saturn throws delays in your path. Think of these as tests of your resolve rather than insurmountable obstacles.

4) *Compromise.* With Saturn, you usually have to give something to get something. Accept the trade-offs that come with Saturnian times, and don't expect a situation where you gain everything and lose nothing. In fact, expect a more or less even trade.

5) *Work.* During a difficult Saturnian break-up, it can help to do that most Saturnian of activities, work. Flying off for a weekend to an island beach is unlikely to be the escape you are hoping for, but if you throw yourself into a work project (and work takes many forms), you will probably find that to be a satisfying way to get a little relief from the grief.

And Now, A Word About Jupiter...

The planet Jupiter has a special place in the process of a break-up, one that is in accord with the basic nature of this beneficent planet. Jupiter transits to any of the key relationship points (Venus, the seventh house, etc.) will rarely coincide with a break-up unless there are also transits by the outer planets. That is, you won't usually see Jupiter initiating a break-up by itself. However, Jupiter has a helpful role to play.

What Jupiter transits do is to help us feel optimistic, a bit bold, and hopeful. If a person has been contemplating a break-up for a while but lacks the courage, self-confidence, or motivation to actually make the change, a transit by Jupiter can help make the change a reality.

For example, Saturn may be squaring the seventh house cusp in a client's chart, an aspect that could highlight his or her desire to be free from the current relationship. Let's say Saturn is in the tenth house by transit, and there is tension between career goals and the relationship, and the latter has not been going very well for some time. We know that Saturn often packs a one-two punch, where with one hand he emphasizes that the partnership has its problems, but with the other gets the person to have doubts about leaving and insecurities about future partnership potential. In other words, Saturn can make it appealing to *play it safe* and *stay with the devil we know.*

The client may be living with the tension for a good part or maybe even all of the 9 months of the Saturn transit, when along comes Jupiter into the seventh house. Suddenly, things begin to look up. Perhaps someone new expresses interest or begins flirting. Or it could be that the client hears a story about someone who is much happier now that they are out of a stale relationship. Or maybe it is just a matter of beginning to feel more confident and have greater faith in life and the potential for meaningful relationships. Ultimately, the Jupiter transit is about greater optimism and faith in the future, whether the person gets outside encouragement or generates the good feelings internally. Thus,

Jupiter can help them to make a move that they would have otherwise hesitated to make. If the client's partner is the one who left, then Jupiter will have the same role of providing optimism about the future, although instead of precipitating the break-up it will have the effect of soothing anxieties about the future. In either case, Jupiter may be in easy or hard aspect to a relationship point, but he can also fulfill his role as cosmic cheerleader by aspecting the sun, moon, or chart ruler (or even his own natal position).

Jupiter will probably not characterize the break-up: that's more typically the four outer planets. But Jupiter can make a difficult situation better, and can help to precipitate changes where there is hesitation, doubt, or a lack of energy. Serious consideration, deep transformation, and other weighty matters are really the key to the process, but sometimes we need to take a leap of faith into the future.

Chapter 11
Going Modal

Going Modal: Assessing the Attitude Towards Change

Nothing is more obvious about a break-up than that it represents a change. Yet we all handle change differently: some of us crave it as a constant source of stimulation, others fear it. How well a person handles the end of a partnership is in many ways determined by their attitude towards change. The moon represents security needs, and so can be very telling about how a person will react to a separation, but other chart factors are important, too. I have found that the modal picture is an excellent way to assess the overall attitude towards change.

Motivation and Movement

In general, we look to the signs the planets are in to assess this basic attitude towards change, what we might call a person's *motivation* for change. We then look to the ascendant and the midheaven in order to assess the speed of change that actually takes place in a person's life, what we might call the degree of *movement* suggested by the chart. These two factors, motivation and movement, can interact in a variety of ways. For example, if they are more or less the same, they can reinforce each other. If motivation and movement are different but in balance, they can complement each other, and if they are different and not in balance, they can antagonize each other.

Getting in the Mode

The three *modes*, cardinal, fixed, and mutable, describe both our motivation for change and the degree of movement. The *cardinal* mode is related to the first month, or first astrological sign (Aries, Cancer, Libra, Capricorn), of each season. It encompasses the energy which begins each season: the first crocuses popping up in springtime as the grass begins to green; the first really hot days of summer; the arrival of crisp autumn air; and the first biting cold of winter. Cardinal energy, for our purposes is *the energy of beginnings*, the energy we use to start things, to initiate. It is a very creative energy, and it moves ahead in a particular direction.

The *fixed* mode is related to the second month, or second astrological sign (Taurus, Leo, Scorpio, Aquarius), of each season. It encompasses the energy which typifies each season: the full bloom of flowers and trees in spring; the intense heat of summer; the golden and fiery red leaves of autumn; the short, snowy days of winter. Fixed energy is *the determination to carry things through*, to endure and to maintain. It moves only slowly, and sometimes appears to stand still.

The *mutable* mode is related to the third month, or third astrological sign (Gemini, Virgo, Sagittarius, Pisces), of each season. It encompasses the energy in which one season begins to turn into the next: when spring lets go into summer as the leaves are on the trees and the days grow longer; as summer wanes into autumn as the days grow shorter and cooler; as autumn transforms into winter, trees standing bare; and as winter gives way to spring, the icy winds replaced by milder breezes. Mutable energy is *flexible and adaptable*. Unlike cardinal energy it does not necessarily have a particular direction.

When we examine motivation and movement, we can see that each can have a dominant mode. Naturally, it is rare to find someone whose motivation is entirely characterized by one mode, and some people can be quite balanced with regard to modal energy.

For *motivation*, I suggest looking at the modes of each of the ten planets and seeing what the distribution is. Some astrologers give more weight to the sun and moon, or have more complex weighting systems, but I prefer to give one point to each planet when looking at the modal picture. I would consider five or more planets in a single mode as a significant indicator of the strength of that mode for the person. Similarly, if two or fewer planets are in a mode, we may begin to think that that mode is somewhat lacking for the person.

When assessing *movement* I look primarily to the angles of the chart. It is common to find that the ascendant and midheaven have the same mode in place to describe the change in a person's life. I also look to see how many planets are in angular, succedent, and cadent houses. Although for relationship purposes we are more concerned with the ascendant-descendant axis and the seventh house, it is worth looking at the MC-IC axis and the associated houses as well. There is no particular formula I use, but I try to balance the house placements with the angles to get an overall view of movement.

The following sections will be a review for many astrologers, but I think it is helpful to understand how I see the modes in operation. You can read this chapter all the way through—doing so will be helpful in making comparisons and contrasts—or you can look up the various combinations as needed.

Cardinal Motivation and Movement

People who have a lot of cardinal motivation tend to get excited about beginnings. You hear them talking about making things happen and they get very into the planning stage of anything.

More than just being excited, however, they are actually comfortable with change and like to begin new things. Usually, they present as real go-getters, with a can-do attitude and an obvious enthusiasm for new things, whether those things are activities or ideas. They tend to get bored with routine and can kind of fade away after projects get started. At work, these people often get everyone fired up for something new, but are quick to move on once the new product is on the shelves or the project is up and running. I know an elementary school principal who likes to go into schools which are running poorly, and in the course of a couple of years turn them around. Then he turns the job over to someone else and finds another school that needs saving. In relationships, the attraction, seduction, and courting phases give cardinal people a charge, while stable, long-term relationships can be more challenging. In a break-up, people with strong cardinal energy may be quick to re-enter the sphere of partnership, and rebound relationships are an obvious possibility.

Cardinal movement means a lot of innovation and change in a person's life. Cardinal movement suggests that a person will begin new relationships and initiate career changes. Cardinal motivation may *want* those things, but cardinal movement gets things to happen. It is important to note that it is not just a matter of change, which can be mutable, but of *initiating* the change. People with cardinal movement push themselves into the game, make things happen, and get things started. They are doers, and rather than passively going along with changes, they impose a direction on things. A cardinal sign on the house of partnership can mean that the person initiates a break-up or seeks to move on quickly if a relationship ends.

Fixed Motivation and Movement
Ah, stability.
People with fixed motivation want to keep things more or less stable. These people have the internal disposition to carry things through. Whether it is work or relationship or any other area of they are ready to shoulder the burden and keep on plugging away.

Routine energizes them, and in the areas of life characterized by fixed energy, they often resist change. Sometimes that resistance is a simple avoidance of any opportunities for change, while at other times it manifests more as a sentimental clinging to the past. Most of us have an area of life which we like to remain more or less stable, and we should remember that the full experience of anything requires that once in a while we stick around long enough to see how things turn out. If a person has strong fixed energy, or fixed energy prevails around relationship planets, a break-up can be a very difficult experience. Look to the moon, Venus, and the sun, especially; but if four or more planets are in fixed signs you can assume that relationship change is welcomed with some hesitation.

Fixed movement is indicated when areas of life don't change for a long period of time. A marriage that really does last until death parts the couple is an example. There are few long-term jobs around any more, although some government jobs still see people staying around long enough to retire. Living in the same area for one's whole life, or a large section of it, is also an example of fixed movement, as is maintaining strong connections to family. Fixed movement might seem a wee bit dull and inimical to the spirit of change, but stability, even if it is really only temporary, is part of the overall cycle of transformation. The full bloom of springtime and the long hot summer days aren't dull, they are a chance to fully appreciate the typical energy of the season. A fixed sign on the house of relationship can make it difficult to initiate the break-up of a partnership, and can mean a protracted process of separation because it is difficult to let go.

Mutable Motivation and Movement

Mutable motivation is almost an oxymoron, since motivation implies *direction* and mutable energy is low on that quality. It is perhaps best to say that people with mutable motivation are *comfortable* with change. They don't mind watching things move from one thing to the next, and accept relatively easily that nothing lasts forever. While people with cardinal motivation often become bored with routine, people with mutable motivation usually manage to avoid getting too caught up in day-to-day ruts. Even if they show up at the same job for year after year, it doesn't seem to faze them, and neither will it faze them if they have to go looking for another job after all those years. It is the same with relationships, in which people with mutable energy often appear to be at least a little detached. When a separation occurs, mutable motivation is often accepting of the change (whether they initiate it or not), and is ready to move into the next stage of life. In contrast to people with lots of cardinal energy, these folks may not have a particular direction in mind.

Mutable movement is easier to see and understand, as it manifests as a great deal of change in a person's life. Someone who moves from one job to another or one relationship to another is usually expressing mutable movement. Unlike cardinal movement, these people don't so much seek out change as respond to new situations as they arise. When this type of energy is particularly high, some people will not only move sequentially but also simultaneously. In the area of relationship, it may be more in tune with mutable movement to date several people on a more or less casual basis, or to have a serious partnership but also have side relationships. People whose movement is mutable sometimes complain that they feel that they are just drifting along, and at an extreme that can be the case. However, people with this characteristic often live lives that are interesting and very rich in experience. During a relationship break-up, the person with mutable movement will generally go with the flow, although the challenge is to avoid falling into a kind of doldrums where nothing much occurs. If you look at the history of some people with mutable relationship energy, you may find that they have had two or more significant partnerships, but these may be followed by years without really connecting with another person on an intimate level.

Combinations of Motivation and Movement

Since there are three modes that describe both motivation and movement in our lives, there are nine possible combinations. Let's take a look at each combination and see how it might work out for an individual. Obviously, each of these nine combinations can manifest in an infinite number of ways, and I'm giving you only the sketchiest outlines of each, with a tiny hint about how relationships may appear. After that, we'll see how each mode deals with the four different outer planet styles of change.

Cardinal Motivation/Cardinal Movement

This combination is obviously very active and is generally tolerant of a high degree of change, so much so, in fact, that boredom can be a very big problem. People with this configuration are comfortable with change, as long as they are the ones initiating it. When it seems like other people, or circumstances, are dictating the changes, they can really bristle against them. A high degree of independence is needed, and it tends to be important for these folks to feel that they are getting their way in a situation. When this person initiates a break-up, they may feel it is a simple matter, over and done quickly, while if his or her partner leaves, it can be more stressful. In either case, moving on quickly is probably the strategy that will be employed.

Cardinal Motivation/Fixed Movement

This can be a frustrating combination. The internal attitude is one of wanting to initiate and begin things, yet life tends to move too slowly in comparison with the person's motivation. Often people with this kind of energy find themselves in leadership positions, which is a good way to use the active cardinal energy within the context of an enduring situation. In relationships, they would probably want to maintain a degree of excitement, which can be difficult over the long run. A good expression of this would be to try new and different activities with the partner, while a less-good alternative would be to constantly stir up emotional issues as a means of keeping things interesting. A separation from the partner may be viewed as either a long-awaited relief or an affront to the person's power and sense of stability.

Cardinal Motivation/Mutable Movement

Things can go either way with this energetic picture. On the one hand, the cardinal and mutable energies are both more or less oriented to change, but on the other hand mutable energy lacks the direction which is characteristic of the cardinal mode. People with this energy sometimes put out a great deal of effort, but somehow have little to show for it. They bring enthusiasm and energy to everything they do, yet rewards never seem to match up to their output. An example of this can be seen in a client who worked her way up the ladder in a company—only to have it close less than a year after she got the keys to the executive washroom. In relationships, the initial enthusiasm for a new romance can fail to lead to an enduring partnership. During a break-up, there may be a desire to move on, but some difficulty gaining the traction needed to make the transition, as with someone who wants to leave a relationship but is held in place by economic circumstances.

Fixed Motivation/Cardinal Movement

This combination can lead to *reluctant success*. The inner desire for stability is countered by a tendency for movement and change in life circumstances, which can be somewhat stressful and a little bewildering. Although it can be difficult, the tendency for cardinal movement at least imposes a direction on things, and the inner motivation for stability helps to balance out the cardinal push for change, often resulting in a very successful combination of determination and direction. In relationships, this combination can make it very easy to attract new partners, while the sought-after long-term relationship can be a bit hard to maintain. Inner hesitation can slow outer progress in relationships. An active partnership where there are a lot of shared interests is the best bet for long-term relationships. Couples that work together as a team in addition to being life partners, or who share the same obsession for a hobby or sport, often do very well when this combination is present. In break-ups, there is often a sense that staying together would be ideal, but if circumstances don't merit continued commitment, changes are made.

Fixed Motivation/Fixed Movement

With this combination, the desired stability is attained, for better or for worse. These people are ready to stick with something all the way through, and life gives them many opportunities to entrench themselves. The only problem with this is that life can become more *stuck* than stable, so that any change at all might be avoided, and that when change does come (as it inevitably does) it can be seen as a threat or a disaster. People in a lasting relationship worry about what will happen to them if their partner dies or leaves, although there are not signs of either happening any time soon. The problem with this combination is that no matter how stable life is, change always will arrive at some point and in the back of our minds we all know it, and that can lead to anxiety. Separations can be seen as disasters, or worse, as *failures*. Despite the craving for stability (and its attainment in many cases), people with this configuration will sometimes initiate separations, particularly when a sought-after goal or deeply help principle is not attained. Even limitation has its limits, after all.

Fixed Motivation/Mutable Movement

Here, the desire to put down roots is strong, but stability always seems elusive. While fixed motivation with cardinal movement usually pulls or pushes a person into new ventures and moves them in a specific direction, the mutable movement of this combination can result in things slipping away without any particular purpose. Let's say a person would like to get married and settle down, but he or she can't find a partner who shares the same goals. Holding to idealized versions of things is another way that fixed motivation can manifest, and people with this combination often feel frustrated when the world fails to live up to the standards they have set. In a break-up, it is important to note whether the person appears to be reacting as a victim of

141

circumstances (mutable overwhelming fixed) or if they are more determined to persevere in spite of changing conditions.

Mutable Motivation/Cardinal Movement

People with mutable motivation can be remarkably flexible, sometimes to the point that to others it can seem peculiar how little they are bothered by life's ups and downs. With this combination, there is rarely much in the way of ambition in the affected areas of life, and sometimes a more laid back attitude is sought. However, the cardinal movement pulls these people forward. Like their fixed motivation/cardinal movement cousins, they can be somewhat reluctant to participate in the opportunities life offers, although they differ in that mutable/cardinal people don't always have the stick-to-it-ness to really accomplish something grand and may duck out when the opportunity arises. In relationships, change may be frequent and often initiated by the person from within, although they can also go for long periods of time in a suitably dynamic relationship. Things often move fast in a break-up, and that's usually the preferred way of handling things for these folks.

Mutable Motivation/Fixed Movement

Once again, the basic flexibility of mutable motivation serves these people well. Change is okay for those with mutable motivation, but so is stability. While cardinal motivation can feel frustration in the context of fixed movement, mutability allows a more laid-back approach. Variations in routine and new opportunities are greeted with enthusiasm, but the day-to-day world is rarely seen as boring or oppressive. To others, in fact, it sometimes appears that people with mutable motivation simply don't care all that much, although being easy-going doesn't really mean being uncaring. At best, they probably make the most out of just about any situation, or at least they think they do. In relationships, the trick is to be sure that they get what they need. If their wants and needs aren't being met, however, they might start to drift out of the relationship on an emotional level, whether or not they actually do anything about it. Once again, a

142

separation can sometimes be seen as relief, a way out of a stagnant situation.

Mutable Motivation/Mutable Movement

As with the other double combinations, there isn't a lot of stress experienced when both motivation and movement are mutable. This lack of stress can have a down side, when the person feels he or she is just drifting along. With this combination, life changes frequently, and that's just fine, most of the time. *Indecision* can be the problem with this combination, and at worst can result in a *failure to launch* kind of scenario. In relationships, too, it is an open question as to whether this combination will lead to a rich history of intimacy or a string of unsatisfying relationships. A long-term partnership usually requires a great deal of flexibility and lots of breathing room when one of the partners has this combination. Break-ups can of course be stressful in themselves, but they are rarely seen as unthinkable or impossible to move beyond.

These nine combinations of motivation and movement represent basic patterns, but at no other point in this book have I so simplified things, and you have to allow for a lot of leniency in reading these descriptions. Remember that even in a single area of life like career or relationship it is rare for someone to be an extreme example of only one of these combinations. Many, many, factors are involved in complicating and enriching these simple summaries. You probably know a few people who are really typical of one of these combinations in some area of their life, but most of us don't quite match up exactly with any of these combinations.

Let's now turn our attention to how each of the three modes responds to the four outer planets. Naturally, there are again myriad possible ways to respond, and an infinite number of specific examples—astrology teaches us that each situation is unique, that no two moments in time are ever exactly the same. As we also know, we can respond in a more or less positive way to each challenge as it arises, and no outcome is ever assured. What we can look at is the general approach to change that each mode takes as the four transit styles present themselves. That will at least give us clue as to how they will handle break-ups that are characteristic of each planet.

Cardinal Energy and Uranian Change

All other things being equal, and they won't be, cardinal energy deals fairly well with Uranian change. The *change* aspect of Uranian times goes down well enough with people who have cardinal motivation, but what can be a bit more challenging is that the direction is not always under their control. The sudden shifts that Uranus indicates work well with a tendency for beginning new things, but when the direction of change is determined by forces outside of the person, there can be considerable resistance, at least for a time. With break-ups, things move fast and with a detached, unemotional flavor when the person initiates, but there can be explosions internally and externally if the sudden shift comes from the partner.

Cardinal Energy and Neptunian Change

This is combination can be a difficult one. Neptunian change is the very antithesis of the focused direction which cardinal energy wants, in terms of both motivation and movement. Neptune takes you on a journey, often of a cruise-to-nowhere variety, while cardinal energy would much prefer a business trip, or at least a safari—something with a destination and a purpose. During Neptunian times, people with cardinal motivation can feel out of sorts as they have difficulty finding their direction, and the doldrums of Neptune can be especially irritating for people with cardinal energy, who are used to *something* happening, and sooner rather than later.

Neptunian change can be a real learning experience for those with strong cardinal energy, and if the experience is strong and significant enough, it can be the first time in their lives that cardinal people feel that they are unable to take some kind of action. The valuable learning experience here is to understand

144

that we cannot be in control of everything that happens, and that once in a while we need to let go and just see what happens.

On the other hand, sometimes cardinal energy is directed by Neptunian enthusiasm. Give cardinal people a guiding myth, and watch them go! With Neptune, it's possible that cardinal energy can be directed towards an illusion, and when that happens people with cardinal motivation are among those most likely to give too much of themselves for a (sometimes lost) cause.

Applied to break-ups, the central question is whether the person is lost at sea, drifting on a raft, or if they at least have a paddle in the water and are moving towards something. Although an outsider may see that goal is illusory or inflated, movement is crucial to cardinal people, and deflating a myth should be done cautiously if at all.

Cardinal Energy and Plutonian Change

Difficult Plutonian times are difficult for everyone: there's no way to make death and rebirth easy, regardless of your attitude towards change. Cardinal motivation can make for a very intense Plutonian obsession of the "gotta have it" variety. In the area of relationships, the person may leave one partner—which can be very difficult—but find a new partner who helps to create a much more intense emotional (and probably sexual) relationship. The powerful energies of the cardinal mode and Pluto are a challenging mixture, to be sure. However, there is often a great deal of creativity released during these times.

Cardinal Energy and Saturnian Change

This scenario suggests frustration, a situation that I describe as being something along the lines of jamming down on the accelerator while the parking break is on. It should be obvious that the tendency towards cardinal motivation is going to be at odds with Saturn's delays and seemingly endless testing. Yet while Saturnian change is quite opposed to the *speed* of cardinal energy, it can have a positive effect on the other aspect of being cardinal, *direction*. When a separation occurs, cardinal people bristle against the slowness of the process, but often engage in it fully. For example, the ongoing proceedings and legalities of a divorce can seem a terrible drag, but under this combination the person is very likely to make the most of the situation, perhaps by working closely with their lawyer. The potential for successful rebuilding in the next phase of life is also suggested by this combination.

Fixed Energy and Uranian Change

Don't get me wrong—Uranian change can be the best thing that ever happens to someone with lots of fixed energy. The problem is that they probably won't *like* it all that much. Fixed energy wants things to stay the same, and Uranus is anything but helpful if it is stability you crave. The same events which might not seem too far out for a person with a cardinal or mutable emphasis can be perceived as devastating when seen through the eyes of a fixed person. Fixed movement means that things don't change all that much, and many times this can mean going from *routine* to *rut* all too easily. Uranian change can be a kind of antidote, a remedy for too much sameness. The disruptive influence of Uranus is usually in proportion to the amount of initial stability we have prior to the transit, and with fixed energy, that amount is usually pretty high. In fact, stability can sometimes become just plain crusty, and a shock from Uranus can be just what the doctor ordered.

Because fixed energy is so much about stability, there can be a tendency to rush through the process of change in order to get to a new state of relative equilibrium. Sometimes, the initial shock has barely registered at all before the person starts to seek some new form of stability. While fixed energy can pretty much guarantee that some form of consistent structure will return, the desire for stability combined with Uranian impulsiveness can result in taking the first option which presents itself, and that can prevent a person from finding a truly higher level of reorganization. In fact, it can sometimes result in accepting a lower level of organization: becoming less complex and having less internal cohesion. Taking the first opportunity that presents itself can short-circuit the process of change and the growth that it offers. In relationships, this would of course be the famous rebound relationship. By contrast, if people with fixed energy can stay open long enough and avoid grasping at apparent stability, they typically can find their way to a very different but certainly stable place. Incorporating some of the Uranian experience into their perspective can be very helpful, as stable periods come to be seen as temporary plateaus rather than eternal resting places.

Fixed Energy and Neptunian Change

Uranus may lead to an "any port in a storm" attitude, but Neptune leaves us lost at sea, in a dense fog, and no port is available. The Neptunian style of change can be especially disorienting for people with a fixed orientation, who would often rather hold on to an unpleasant situation than let go into any kind of uncertainty. Neptunian change is the very opposite of fixedness—it is a time when nothing seems certain, an extended chaos shrouded in dense fog. But that fog can work wonders.

Neptunian change can soften the hard lines of fixed energy. Like the fog that penetrates concrete pillars so that moss can grow on them, or the steam that penetrates wood so that it can be bent into a new shape, Neptunian change can introduce softness and pliability to fixed energy. What has to change is the rigid demand for *sameness*, while the desire for *consistency* can remain, and people can learn to see how the same principles can apply in a variety of situations.

In relationships, the fixed demand for sameness can reach a fevered pitch, as any change is seen as signs of possibly losing the partner. Through the process of Neptunian change, handled well, they might be able to accept a more flexible approach to relationships—even if it costs the present partnership to learn the lesson.

Fixed Energy and Plutonian Change

Fixed energy tends to view significant change with trepidation and anxiety, and no change is as deep as Plutonian change. The solid structures fixed energy likes to build are no match for the forces of Pluto, just as the stone buildings of Pompeii were no match for Vesuvius.

Once again, Plutonian change can be an effective antidote for too much fixed energy. The problem with is that fixed energy tends to want to control or prevent change, and Pluto isn't about to turn over the steering wheel. After the initial pain of the breakdown and uncertainty, however, fixed people are usually infused with the energy of Pluto. The structures they rebuild in their lives have a certain power that is characterized by a subtle kind of flexibility. Duration comes to mean maintaining direction in the midst of change rather than resisting transformation. Plutonian break-ups are hard on people with fixed energy, yet "that which doesn't kill me makes me stronger" (although that only works if it *doesn't* kill you).

Fixed Energy and Saturnian Change

As you probably have realized, fixed energy isn't especially comfortable with change. *Fixed*, after all, implies minimal change. At best, people with fixed energy can manage to become like giant redwoods, enduring and growing while remaining calm and centered as the forest changes around them. Of course, that is much easier said than done.

But Saturn is all about structure, and Saturnian change tends to be slow, so is this the exception to the rule? Yes and no. For one thing, although Saturn doesn't usually signal rapid changes, he does signal change and any change can be a threat to the status quo. Saturn also has a knack of hitting us where we feel uncomfortable and vulnerable, so that even a minor change can cause anxiety. On the other hand, it is also the case that Saturn builds structures and can limit our movement, something to which fixed energy can respond well. In relationships, Saturn might mean marriage, a welcome event for those craving stability. Many times, relationships that could and perhaps should fall apart are held together by the arrival of a baby. I have deep doubts about how healthy this is for anyone involved, particularly the child, but the addition of a new responsibility is a very Saturnian way of ensuring fixed people stay in the same place. The matter-of-fact quality of Saturnian break-ups makes them slightly more palatable to people with fixed energy than transitions that are described by the other outer planets.

Mutable Energy and Uranian Change

Mutable energy does fairly well with change, even the shocks and bumps of Uranian change. The secret is the inherent flexibility of mutable energy. But having a mutable emphasis in motivation or movement doesn't mean being like one of those clown-faced punching bags that keep popping back to the same position no matter how hard you hit them. A better image is the kind of pine tree that grows close to the shore, usually on a windy rock. Pines are pretty flexible, and they bend in the wind. Constant wind results in the famous wind-swept pine that looks like it is billowing in the breeze, even when none is blowing. Change affects mutable people, transforming them. It just doesn't *bother* them all that much.

The shocks of Uranian change are not always welcome, but mutable people are generally able to get themselves back on track fairly quickly after the disruption. Because they aren't uncomfortable with change, the initial phase is usually seen as a signal that it is time to move on. Uranian change is something of a challenge to people with lots of mutable motivation or movement, but it represents a period in which the changes they are used to continue to happen, but with more intensity.

Mutable Energy and Neptunian Change

Neptune's energy strongly resembles mutability to begin with, so this style of change can feel like *more of the same*. While Uranus represents change sped up for mutable people, Neptunian change represents a higher degree of uncertainty than mutable people are used to. Mutable energy suggests moving from one thing to the next easily, yet Neptune can mean moving from one thing to *no thing*. After a while, questions start to emerge about where the person is going. In other words, mutable people might be used to or at least feel comfortable with being bounced around from place to place, but Neptune can mean being knocked off course and drifting in no particular direction. That can be a bit unsettling for people who are used to landing *somewhere* (even if they don't choose the specific location).

Sometimes, Neptune certainly does provide a direction, in the form of a guiding myth or an illusion to be chased. If that's the case, people with a lot of mutability in their motivation or movement may overcompensate for having had little determination and direction in the past. There is a possibility that they can go a little overboard, certain that they've found *the* thing, whether that is a relationship, a guru, or a job. Used with a bit of awareness, however, the presence of an inspiring vision can help to provide motivation for those who feel they have a lack of direction.

Mutable Energy and Plutonian Change

Even the flexibility and adaptability of mutable energy can be challenged by Plutonian change. Part of the profile of strong mutability is that it often can prevent a person from going too deep into anything. People with a lot of mutable energy can sometimes seem to flit from one thing to another, having many surface experiences without really exploring any one thing in any real depth. Pluto can help to fix that problem by bringing the focus to an area of life and maintaining it through a significant transformation.

Mutable flexibility usually helps a person to move through the changes with less resistance than the other modes. While it doesn't necessarily make for a pleasant experience, at least it is not felt to be a complete disaster. Of course, when the changes are framed in a more positive light, such as the birth of a wanted child, the person with a lot of mutable energy will move through the changes with a general ease that can help them to enjoy the experience.

When people with a strong tendency for mutable movement go through Plutonian changes, they often emerge visibly changed. They may appear and feel somewhat older, but it is more to the point to say that they are *wizened* by the experience. In all probability, they will maintain their flexible attitude towards life and continue to move more or less easily with its changes.

However, they now have a greater sense of direction and purpose, and the changes seem to be leading them somewhere instead of just taking them on a tour of various ways of being. It is as though they move themselves to the center hub of a revolving wheel, having found a centered place in the midst of change. That is often very obvious when relationships are the affected area of life. Someone who has moved from one relationship to another without much concern can begin to feel the profundity that the loss of a partner can be.

Mutable Energy and Saturnian Change

When Saturnian change operates on mutable energy, the tendency is to slow down the pace of change. Usually, Saturn's influence does not last that long, and that makes it easier for those with mutable energy to slow down for a bit. It's also true that Saturn likes us to make decisions and choices, and this can be the irritating part of the process for people who like to stay open and flexible. If you'd like to remain uncommitted in a relationship, Saturnian change is likely to feel like an imposition at one point or another.

Saturn's effect on mutable movement is a little more ambiguous. Here, he tends to slow down the process of change and create a stable situation, at least for a time. Saturn often slows things down and allows structure to develop, even in the mutable signs. Sometimes, this change really is long lasting, while sometimes it only appears to be so.

The key to dealing with Saturnian change for people with mutable energy is to pay close attention to the choices being offered and to choose carefully. During a break-up, the question may be whether the person with mutable energy is ready to make the choice—that can be the difference between emerging stronger from the process and feeling like a victim.

Once again, the profiles in this chapter represent greatly simplified images of the three modes. Most people display a complex composite of the modes in their astrological charts and in their lives, and the specifics of the planets and houses involved add depth to the generalities I have presented. However, it is also true that in a relationship ending, the astrologer may see that one mode really dominates the process. Understanding how cardinal, fixed, and mutable energy respond to change can be very helpful at times when significant transitions are occurring. It is a good strategy to use the ideas in this chapter to probe around and see how the client is feeling, rather than to make assumptions and tell them how they feel. In the end, the greatest benefit may be in the astrologer's own understanding of the internal and external dynamics of the situation.

Chapter 12
Generations

As a rule, clients don't like to hear about generational considerations in an astrological consultation. Perhaps they will listen when they are seeking advice about a life path or other big picture things, but when something like relationship or career comes up, I find that very few clients are inclined to take the generational perspective into account. Much of this chapter is, therefore, for the astrologer's benefit, to help fill in your perspective.

Each astrological generation has certain responsibilities, particular issues they are helping us to work out. Awareness of the generational aspect of our lives is really very helpful if we can embrace it—it removes some of the personal pressure, and it can help to alleviate the sense of guilt that many people feel around issues. Knowing that we have a particular mission and a role to play can help to contextualize our personal experiences and see meaning in our struggles. It also helps to know that we're not alone in some of the challenges that we face. Still, there is quite a bit of resistance to seeing personal issues in a collective context, and astrologers need to be aware of that.

The overall pattern of generational issues is fairly straightforward, at least until you begin to look into the complex ways that it manifests. There are two sides to the generational picture. On the one hand, there are the events that happen when a planet is in a given sign. For those years, everyone—no matter when they were born—tends to focus on the related issues. On the other hand, people who are born when a planet is in a particular sign tend to carry the debates, beliefs, and changes that occurred at that time forward throughout their lives.

For example, during the Great Depression when Pluto was in the sign of Cancer, the entire world dealt with a crisis in which there was a lack of food and resources were scarce. Those who were alive during the Depression, in one way or another were aware of it and had to deal with it, whether they were ten or ninety years old. You may notice, however, that the people who were born during that time tend to be very focused on money, and particularly food, regardless of their individual fortunes (which obviously vary considerably). Whether by being very frugal or by surrounding themselves in luxury, they usually have a very definite attitude towards wealth and material possessions, and this is true regardless of the circumstances of their birth. Being born into poverty or a well-to-do family has little effect on whether they place extra emphasis on finances later in life. So, everyone deals with the issues that arise at the time the outer planet is in a sign, but the generation born at that time carries those issues forward throughout their lives. It is as though the concerns are announced as the planet goes through the sign, and everyone begins to work on it. Then the people who are born at that time continue the work, although in the background much of the time, because as time goes on we focus on new topics.

Earlier in life, the issues of each generation tend to be more unconscious—they form a constellation of assumptions about life, and although there may be an awareness that others feel differently about the matter, one tends to cleave rather tightly to one's viewpoint. Later in life, as ideas and ideals are given flesh by experience, greater flexibility can develop and one can begin to see many sides to an issue. As a generation gets older, members who have not developed such flexibility may have a rougher time than those who have.

A word about Saturn. You may have noticed that he is left out of the generational picture. That's because he travels a little too fast to really make for what we would call a generation, spending about two and half years in each sign, and while it is possible to see sub-generation similarities among people who have Saturn in the same sign, the effect is not quite as dramatic.

Saturn also represents the boundaries of our personal selves. Uranus, Neptune and Pluto are often referred to as transpersonal planets, meaning that their effect goes beyond our individual sense of self. Saturn sits rights at the boundary of the personal, representing the forces that keep us contained, such as social pressure and family expectations. He is not quite personal, but not quite generational either. To look at it another way, Saturn has to do with those factors that limit and structure us as individuals, while Uranus, Neptune and Pluto have to do with where we are contributing to something beyond the individual self.

In our considerations for this book, I begin with the 1930s. That is somewhat prejudicial for older people, I realize, and it will not help much if you are interested in doing historical analysis. However, people born before the 1930s are now past their third Saturn return, and I am not sure that I have much to offer them in terms of relationship advice. As for doing historical research on famous break-ups, I trust that you will get the idea from what follows and apply it to astrogenerations not specifically considered here.

Plutonian Generations

Pluto in Cancer (1914 – 1939)

Cancer is often thought of as a warm-and-fuzzy sign, and indeed nurturing and caring are a part of the Cancerian picture, but more fundamentally Cancer has to do with the biological needs for individual survival, including food, shelter and clothing.

Cancer is also about having a home base, a clan or group with whom one can feel protected and secure. A typical Cancerian image is that of a baby on its mother's breast, which reflects the energy of this sign at the level of the individual. If we take that same imagery and move it forward in time, the protection and nurturing of the mother becomes the home and the larger family, and the breast becomes the pantry or the kitchen. At another level, it is the clan (or larger community) that protects and provides the means of nourishment for the individual families. At an even more removed level, nations can be seen as having a similar function, and in fact at this level the mother and father are often represented as the queen and king. As we move the symbolism to other levels, the earth itself can be seen as the nourisher and protector of us all, Mother Earth, and so on up to a cosmic level in which the entire universe is pictured as a being birthed from the womb of the Great Goddess.

During the years Pluto was in the sign of Cancer, issues of nurturing and protectiveness were prominent. The Great Depression brought the focus to material goods (*material* comes from *matter* and is related to the word *maternal*, or *mother*). Just as the infant is frightened and hungry if the breast does not produce milk, so people became frightened and hungry when they found their pantries empty. The dust bowl in the United States during that era was an example of the earth herself going dry and failing to produce food.

Just as a hungry infant might become impatient with her mother when no milk is coming, the depression had political consequences as people began to demand more from their governments. The result was that some very extreme forms of government such as communism and fascism arose or became more fanatical. With the sense that resources were limited, clans (in this case, nations) began to see each other as enemies, facilitating the Second World War. Actually though, no such motivation was needed, as the First World War, before the Depression, also took place with Pluto in Cancer.

Those born with Pluto in Cancer include the Depression Babies I described earlier. As a group, they tend to be either very

156

patriotic (many who were born early in the generation fought in the Second World War) or to have a strong allegiance to some group, such as a political party. But they also have been working on transcending such boundaries, and were instrumental in setting up the European Common Market and later the European Union.

In terms of relationship and endings, this group struggles with the boundaries. Many of the Pluto in Cancer generation resist the idea marriage or relationship outside of ethnic or religious groups, and progressive movements like gay marriage had little chance when this generation had the greatest political power. Significantly, many Pluto/Cancer folks were also brought up with deep resistance to divorce. The need for security can be very high with this group, and although some members of this generation were trailblazers in breaking the rules of social convention (especially if those also born with Uranus in Aries), divorce can be a sore spot even today.

Pluto in Leo (1937 – 1958)

Oh, those Baby Boomers! Leo is the sign of the child, the ego, and of royalty, and the Pluto in Leo generation put the very idea of being *a generation* on the map, as though the entire cohort was determined to be a star among generations.

Earlier generations, like Pluto in Cancer, were not always all that enthusiastic about the Boomers, labeling them the *Me Generation*. There is something to that, as the Pluto-in-Leo generation was intent on showing their value as individuals, and they were quick to question both authority and tradition. They are a generation which values the individual more than the collective, and which emphasizes that each individual is special.

As Leo is the sign of the child, this group has been resistant to aging. If you look at a picture of thirty-year olds from the 1930s or 1950s, you see *adults*. But look at the Baby Boomers as they round sixty or seventy, and you see that youthful gleam in their eyes.

Members of this generation are unlikely to accept the status quo and sit quietly when relationship issues emerge. The

157

emphasis on the individual's value and the freedom to blaze a path for oneself is paramount, and this generation was the one that began to take advantage of the liberalized divorce laws in the 1970s. Yet it would be wrong to imply that love and relationship is not a prominent concern for this generation, as it is actually one of the most romantically inclined of all astro-generations. Balancing the needs of the individual with those of the partner has been a long struggle of the Boomers, and they have done well with this difficult issue.

Pluto in Virgo   (1958 – 1972)

The years when Pluto was in Virgo were the tumultuous 1960s, and at first glance it may appear that the generation born at this time did not carry the revolutionary energy of that time forward in any obvious way. Yet this generation redefined what it is to work (a form of service), effectively putting an end to the lifetime career with a single employer, and moving the criteria for employment to one which is based more on demonstrable skills like being able to program a computer, than on title and degree.

Members of this generation should take a little time to think about where in their life they have found something or someone that is more important than personal gain. They might also consider where have they flatly refused to play the game, keeping true to an ideal rather than copping out.

The Pluto in Virgo generation is a benefactor of the two prior generations, who fought out the battle of tradition and culture versus the individual. By the time Pluto in Virgo came of age, new lines had already been drawn and an armistice reached, at least for a time. This generation accepts that relationships may end, and may even raise an eyebrow of skepticism to think that in the recent past one really did marry until parted by death, no matter how one felt about it. The relationship challenge for this cohort is to experience partnership rather than think about it, and to process rather than analyze relationship changes.

Pluto in Libra   (1972 – 1984)

When I was in the sixth grade, it seemed there wasn't a week when some classmate didn't come in and announce that his parents were splitting up, or that some new kid would arrive in our town with her recently divorced mother. It was the 1970s, and Pluto was in Libra, the sign of relationships.

This was the time when divorce laws were liberalized across the Western world, and the divorce rate skyrocketed as unhappy couples took advantage of the opportunity to start over. It was also the era of experimental relationships, like open marriage and communal marriage. Gay people came into the public, refusing to be closeted any longer. While people had long lived together before marriage, "living in sin," as it was often called, finally became an accepted middle class lifestyle. The changes to relationship structure during the Pluto-in-Libra years were deep, and while the more experimental ideas may have faded from the headlines, we continue to redefine partnership as this era reverberates through the decades.

People born at this time sit on one side of the fence or the other. Many members of this generation literally crave a monogamous, traditional relationship, although they sometimes have a hard time finding one. Other Pluto-in-Libra people are very comfortable breaking the relationship mold, and either eschew traditional relationships altogether, or settle into them only after a long period of experimentation. Many of the things that were fiercely debated during the 1970s, such as living together without marriage and open relationships, are taken for granted by much of this generation. The great taboo against homosexuality has fallen away like dust on a windy day, and casual encounters between members of the same sex are neither uncommon nor secret.

Members of the Pluto-in-Libra generation should review their ideas and assumptions about relationships, and see how these have fit into their actual lifestyles. While career and other areas of life are of course affected by the various styles of change, members of this generation will feel especially affected when it is relationships that are in the midst of change. Whether that is good news or not depends on attitudes towards both partnership and change itself.

Pluto in Scorpio (1984 – 1995)

For a while there, sex was just fun. With Pluto (and Uranus— we'll get to him in a bit) shaking up relationships in the 1970s, and sexuality already liberalized by the availability of birth control (Neptune—have patience), the decade became kind of an orgy in some quarters.

One day in the very early 1980s, I saw an old high school acquaintance at a party, a gay man I knew through the drama club. He seemed to be a little stoned on something, not quite making any coherent statements, which I didn't think was all that unusual. What was unusual were the two purple rashes that decorated his cheeks, making him look a little like a mustached Raggedy Andy. None of us knew it at the time, but he was the first we were seeing of a new disease that would change our attitudes about sexuality for our lifetime. AIDS had arrived.

Scorpio is ruled by Pluto, and both are associated with sex, birth, and death. Pluto certainly packed a wallop during his brief visit to his home sign. It is hard to imagine the fear which spread when people learned that if they had had sex during the last five or so years with anyone who had had sex within the last five or so years with someone who was infected (or had had sex within the last five years with someone...) that they might have an incurable and deadly disease. Talk about an unexpected turn in the Sexual Revolution!

Sex wasn't the only thing that could kill you, of course. There were tainted needles used with intravenous drugs, which a surprising number of people had tried at one time or another. And then there was health care. Were the needles really clean? Was the blood supply being tested? What about the equipment at the dentist's office? The tools at the nail salon? We even worried about a walk on the beach, for used hypodermic needles from hospital trash were washing onto the shore: what if you stepped on one? For the time Pluto was in Scorpio, it seemed that life itself could kill you. Pluto reminded us that our biology matters, that despite all of our advances in technology and medicine, our bodies still walk a slippery slope, and all of our ideas, beliefs, loves, feelings, and emotions are tied to those bodies.

The generation born while Pluto was in Scorpio shows a tendency towards the gothic. They are surprisingly comfortable on the dark side of things, as a rule, although some of that may be down to style more than substance. It is the Pluto in Scorpio generation that finds vampires—who are, after all, dead people—sexy. They are the generation that gets pierced and tattooed early in life, as though the future may not matter. In fact, they seem to be saying that the future may not get here at all.

Following the lead of Pluto-in-Leo, subsequent generations have made an extended childhood for themselves and their children, while the Scorpions have arrived on this planet ready to deal with the hard facts. More ready, in fact than any generation has ever been. It remains to be seen how these folks deal with relationship endings, and of course there is incredible variety within any generation, but it seems likely that this generation will actively redefine commitment and break through existing limitations. This generation wants commitment, but it must be real, soul-based commitment if it is to last. That is both a noble aspiration and rather steep climb for mortals.

Pluto in Sagittarius (1995 – 2009)

If you were around during most of the 20th century, the idea that religion would be a major factor in world politics probably seemed absurd. Even the religious conflicts that were around were widely attributed not to belief but to economics, with many people assuming that religion was just covering up more earthly concerns. Then Pluto marched into Sagittarius, the sign of religion, beliefs, and philosophy, and we learned that we weren't quite so over these things after all.

For those of us who thought that religion and cultural beliefs weren't powerful enough to motivate people any longer, September 11th, 2001 was a dramatic and gruesome wake-up call. But the Pluto-in-Sagittarius years were full of controversy centering on religious beliefs. The science-versus-religion wrestling match over evolution is one example, where each side insisted on dumbing-down the other until the argument was as trivial as it was heated. Despite these dramatic examples, what was perhaps most striking about these years was the number of people who became seriously religious, and the large number who became religious fundamentalists. Yet there was also a great expansion of New Age and alternative spirituality, which went from esoteric bookshops to filling a large section in major bookstores. Spiritually oriented films such as *The Secret* also penetrated into popular culture. Even within the world of traditional religion, there was a great crossing of cultural boundaries, and for every Christian who joined a fundamentalist church, it seemed there was another who joined a Buddhist sangha.

We are just beginning to see this generation within the context of relationship, and haven't had much opportunity to see how they will handle break-ups. Since beliefs are such a big part of the Sagittarian picture, we can expect to see some members of this generation will return to very traditional models of relationship— prescribed by religion in many cases—at least for a time. On the other hand, the equally Sagittarian sense of exploration and expansion will probably yield new models of relationship and a greater tolerance for changes within a relationship.

Pluto in Capricorn (2008 – 2024)

Capricorn is the sign of the institution, the government, and the corporation. Deep changes in the economy and the way that it is structured are clearly part of these years, and those born at this time will carry those changes forwards in their lives. In terms of relationship it is clear that an acceptance of new models, such as gay marriage, is part of Pluto in Capricorn, but we may also see that the resistance to change takes root in some members of this generation.

Neptunian Generations

Neptune in Virgo (1928 – 1943)

Remember that Neptune inspires an almost spiritual devotion to something, and you can imagine how Neptune affected the sign of service. Much of the male population of the world was in uniform during these years, and the ideal of service was very, very strong. The willingness of people to give their lives for ideals—whether those ideals were lofty or crackpot—was at an extreme. Early members of the Pluto-in-Leo generation have Neptune in Virgo, and they were among those who set the idealistic tone for the 1960s.

The generation born at this time was among the first to raise questions about military conscription, and they also started to rebel against the authoritarian structure of the workplace. Of course, they were just as likely to be proud defenders of tradition, at work and elsewhere.

The Neptune in Virgo generation needs to consider how they try to live up to ideals, and the potential dangers of putting others' concerns above their own. In terms of relationship, the question is also one of service and deciding when one is giving too much to a relationship.

Neptune in Libra   (1943 – 1957)

Father comes home from his day at the office, newspaper tucked under his arm. He waves to the children who are playing in the driveway, and walks through the front door. Inside, he is greeted by his beautiful wife, who has a big smile waiting for him. They kiss, and maybe she fixes him a drink. They are happy. Their family is happy. The whole world is happy.

If this sounds like a scene from an old black-and-white sitcom you used to watch, you're right on target. The Neptune-in-Libra years were a time when relationships were idealized, and they were seen as the center of the society. Of course, it wasn't only middle-American ideas about an ideal relationship that were in circulation. All kinds of romantic images flourished during this era, as they have through all eras. What changed was the significance attached to these images.

The generation born at this time, which overlaps with a large part of the Pluto-in-Leo/Baby Boom generation, really idealized love. As they reached their teens and twenties, they were the generation of love-ins, whose anthem was *All You Need is Love*. At times, the spiritualizing power of Neptune helped this generation to see beyond personal, romantic love towards a more universal connection with all beings, yet at other times they seemed to work on the faith that finding *the one*, a soul mate, was really the key to happiness. When Pluto and Uranus went through Libra in the 1970s, this generation reacted in two ways. Some members retreated towards the traditional and made a conscious effort to settle down, while others led the vanguard for change in relationships.

For member of this generation, relationship changes will be very significant. When break-ups occur, they should consider how they handled these changes back in the 1970s, and how they want to respond to them today. Do they welcome or fear changes to personal partnerships? Do they have any sense of having gone beyond and transcended the limitations of relationships as they used to define them? Is the ideal of relationship more important than the reality?

Neptunian hopelessness about relationship is a potential pitfall for this astrological cohort. They may feel that they are too old for meaningful partnership (they are not) or that the best relationships are behind them (that isn't necessarily the case). It's important to explore and explode these ideas, because the Neptunian extreme that said, "I can have a perfect relationship" can swing to its opposite and declare, "I can't have any meaningful relationship."

Neptune in Scorpio   (1957 – 1971)

When the planet of idealization (and also drugs) arrived in the sign of sex, the party really got started. Neptune in Scorpio was active on many fronts, but none so much as the arrival of what used to be called simply "The Pill." The sexual revolution may have been simmering under the surface for decades, but it was really a pharmacological invention that fired the shot heard around the world. Things may have reached their peak in the 1970s, but sexuality (Scorpio) really started to go beyond (Neptune) the boundaries during these years.

The generation born with Neptune in Scorpio tends to take sexual liberation for granted, although times aren't what they once were. In fact, this group retreated from the front lines of the revolution when the going got tough, although some members also adapted sexually to changing times. This generation is among the first to be comfortable with pornography, which went from seedy bookshops to mainstream media under their guidance.

As with the prior Neptunian generation, the Scorpions may swing from idealization to hopelessness, only here the emphasis is on sexuality rather than relationship. The sense of being too old for sex will eventually be an issue for some members of this generation (although they are likely to turn to pharmaceutical solutions if they encounter actual physical limitations). Retiring from sexuality to a celibate life is not necessarily the most constructive option for this generation.

Neptune in Sagittarius   (1970 – 1984)

This era was characterized by a kind of *intense mellowness* as dreamy Neptune passed through high-flying Sagittarius. Rock music went from three minute songs to entire album sides devoted to a single track. Cannabis was on the verge of legalization, and was decriminalized in many places. Every movie had a car chase that lasted 15 minutes, and some movies were pretty much *just* extended car chases. And fads. Fads are always part culture, but the Neptune in Sagittarius era produced them at an unprecedented pace, as we seemed to go overboard in Neptunian fantasy, buying everything from pet rocks to mood rings.

On a deeper level, this was also the era when the many strands of thought that had percolated in the 1960s settled down to become what we now call the New Age. There was a great openness to cross-cultural philosophies and religions. What was to become mainstream when Pluto passed through this sign was in many ways established during Neptune's stay here.

Members of this generation, predictably, either exhibit a great deal of tolerance and flexibility in their beliefs, or they can be among the staunchest defenders of the faith. The Neptune in Sagittarius years also saw the resurgence of fundamentalism and religious conservatism with the Moral Majority, an earlier version of the mindset that was to come when Pluto passed through this sign. The role of this generation, in a sense, is to help us talk out our attitudes about religion and spirituality. Ultimately, we need to recognize that the transcendent and metaphysical can never be put into precise words, so there is no need to fight about our descriptions of god.

Many of our clients will be "spiritual but not religious," and will probably be on the more flexible side of the equation (mainstream religion has little tolerance for astrology), but you never know, and you have to consider that your client's partner may be more fundamentalist. In terms of relationship endings, you are likely to see people who are at least philosophically inclined to accept changes, although they will of course have more personal viewpoints as well.

Should you find someone who is determined to remain in the relationship because they feel that it is the right thing, what God wants, etc., a relationship ending could come with a philosophical crisis. At that point, the individual may be able to adopt a more flexible viewpoint, or they could sink into self-recrimination for failing to live up to their beliefs.

Neptune in Capricorn   (1984 – 1998)

Capricorn is the sign of the institution. Governments and businesses fall under Capricorn, generally speaking, and when Neptune went through this sign, the world changed significantly. The Cold War ended with the dissolution (Neptune) of the Soviet Union and the communist countries of the Eastern Block. Poland led the way, and communism seemed to simply dissolve: it was as though one day it was there, the next it was gone. A world that had become used to dividing itself in two was suddenly changed, and new axes of alignment began to emerge. Of course, it wasn't all that simple. As Tiannamen Square in China demonstrated, some countries became even more hardline. Political and military struggles of course continue, and in a sense one effect of Neptune in Capricorn was the blurring of lines. It was *easy*, after all, when the Iron Curtain separated East and West. The Berlin Wall wasn't good, but no matter which side you were on, you knew who was who. Not so today, with shifting alliances and complex political changes leaving us to wonder which countries really are democracies, and which just say they are.

The people born at this time have varied attitudes towards governments and institutions. In general, they do not appear too interested in politics, and seem to take it for granted that the world operates on the basis of technology and economics more than on politics. In this they may have some insight, although things are perhaps not as open as they think. Most importantly, this astrological cohort was present for the birth of the Internet, the great shared institution run by no one. The net is this generation's model of how things get done.

Capricorn isn't a particularly relationship-oriented sign, so this astro-generation isn't too relevant to break-ups (although of course its members are also members of other astrological generations, such as Pluto in Scorpio). One issue that may emerge for some people in this generation is what gets priority in the struggle between career and relationship. The institution of marriage is likely to get a significant reworking by this generation, as well.

Neptune in Aquarius   (1999 – 2012)

It can be a little hard to imagine there was a time without the Internet, but there was. Neptune's time in Aquarius got just about all of us online, chatting, twittering, friending, and living second lives on our computers. The Internet went from research tool to shopping mall to social gathering place in almost no time. Neptune also got us invested in technology in a more literal way, with the tech stock bubble in the late 1990s. True to Neptune's modus operandi, many of us believed that unlimited growth and

167

expansion were part of a new world order, where none of the old rules applied, an idea which only lasted until the bubble burst.

Members of this generation will have to work with the potentials and pitfalls of technology. It is possible that some of these folks will actually become technophobes, while others simply recognize the value of nature while not entirely rejecting technology. Most of this generation, however, will accept technology and incorporate it into every aspect of their lives, including relationship. While online dating services are the most obvious manifestation we see today, it is quite possible that technology will offer ways to have some of our most significant relationships entirely online—and perhaps with nonhuman computer programs (you already have mixed feelings about the woman on your GPS, don't you?). The basics of communication are already in place, and online sexuality is common. An enhancement or two here and there may make cyber-intimacy the preferred means of connecting with partners soon, and it may become ordinary for this generation. What that will mean for their break-ups, we can only guess.

Uranian Generations

Uranus is a bit of a tough case. It is considered a generational planet, like Neptune and Pluto, yet he spends half as much time in a sign (about seven years) as Neptune, and as little as a quarter of the time that Pluto resides in a sign. What's more, since the last half of the 20th century, he has been in the same part of the zodiac as his slower-moving friends. As we know, Uranus tends to set things off and get them moving, and he has been initiating changes in signs before and after Pluto and Neptune get there.

So, Uranus does count as a generational planet, but for our purposes, it may be most helpful to think about his role as supporting changes that Pluto and Neptune are signaling with their passage through the signs. The Uranian generations have a particular flavor, but it is usually a bit harder to recognize, unless Uranus happens to be in the same sign as one of the other transpersonal planets (which has happened quite often in recent decades). For all these reasons, we'll start with Uranus a little later than we did with Neptune and Pluto.

Uranus in Gemini (1941 – 1949)

These were the years during and immediately after the Second World War, and during this time communication, air travel, and technology took a major leap forward. If you look at the way people were living in the 1930's and compare that with life just a decade later, you can almost feel the difference. When Uranus hit Gemini, the modern world came to Main Street. Of all the profound changes that took place, however, we might be excused for focusing on one little box (although it has rarely been all that little in its history): the television. While it took a few years for televisions to become ubiquitous in living rooms and eventually most other rooms, the first commercial broadcasts took place when Uranus was in Gemini.

Members of this generation are among several that I've discussed in this chapter that would do well to consider their relationship to technology. Specifically, what have we gained and lost in terms of our collective consciousness? Television has connected the entire world, yet it has also isolated us in our homes. This generation tends to be relatively comfortable with new technology, too. Relationship questions might focus on the sense of community and support the person feels during a break-up.

Uranus in Cancer (1949 – 1956)

Just as Pluto in Cancer brought up deep issues about food, home, family, and nation, Uranus moved us in a new direction on these same topics. To put it perhaps too simply, Pluto made us question our relationship to our roots, while Uranus allowed us to experiment and try new ways of living.

Suburban sprawl started in the years after the Second World War, and having one's own kingdom on a half-acre piece of land expressed the royal energy of Pluto in Leo while upending the simple divide between city and country in a Uranian fashion. Many people were quick to realize that a certain Uranian coolness

169

and sterility characterized the new developments, but they offered a new freedom of movement and privacy on a scale previously unimagined. This generation needs to consider: how do they want to live? How do they think people should be living? What is their relationship to food, home, and comfort? How do these things affect their attitudes towards relationship?

Uranus in Leo   (1955 – 1962)

Uranus was in Leo at more or less the same time as Pluto, although Uranus stayed a little longer, more or less extending the Baby Boom generation. Creativity really took off during the Uranus in Leo years, with the birth of Rock and Roll, which combined Uranian rebelliousness with Leonine creativity and a focus on youth. This generation needs to consider the role of creativity in their lives. Who is, and who should be, the stars of their world? In terms of relationship and separation, how do they balance the value of themselves as individuals with the value of partnership, and what is their relationship to social mores about relationship?

Uranus in Virgo   (1961 – 1969)

Uranus and Pluto cruised through the sign of Virgo together in the 1960s, meeting during the middle years of the decade, 1965 and 1966. Uranus added a revolutionary spark to Pluto's deep changes in the areas of service, and the Civil Rights movement inspired many similar movements, the beginning of an era in which diverse groups and individuals began to assert their rights and demand their share of political and social power. Members of this generation need to consider for what ideal they are willing to go to the mat.

In terms of relationship, the question may be whether they put themselves in service to the partnership (or to the partner), and if so whether it is a good decision. The combination of Neptune in Scorpio with Pluto and Uranus in Virgo makes for a group that can seek medical intervention for relationship and sexuality issues, assuming that some pill or procedure can fix anything. On the other hand, as it matures, this generation also is developing a

170

deep suspicion of those approaches and is turning towards alternative medicine and therapy.

Uranus in Libra   (1968 – 1975)

Again, Uranus and Pluto were tag-teaming a sign. Uranus leant his energy to the changes that were discussed in the section on Pluto in Libra. Members of this generation need to have a deep consideration of relationship values. They may fall on the more revolutionary side of the Pluto in Libra generation, although Uranian reversibility can mean that they become very concerned with settling down.

Uranus in Scorpio   (1974 – 1981)

As Uranus cruised through sign of sex and death, he prepared the way for Pluto's time there, which began two years after Uranus left the sign. The openness in relationships that characterized the outer planets in Libra certainly had a sexual side to it, and the late 1970s were a time when many people sought Uranian freedom in sexuality. Neptune's passage through Scorpio had delivered the birth control pill and a greater sense of sexual freedom, but Uranus really pulled out all the stops. If the 1960s were a time of *free love*, the 1970s were all about *free sex*. It was a hedonistic time in many places. But just as Uranus was leaving Scorpio, a conservative wave swept over the Western world, and a previously unknown virus began to spread.

Members of this generation should consider the role that sexuality plays in their lives, their attitudes towards sex, and the relationship between sexuality and love.

Uranus in Sagittarius   (1981 – 1988)

Uranus overlapped with Neptune in Sagittarius for a few years, helping to fuel the extremes of both the Moral Majority and the New Age, two very different visions of religion and spirituality. Members of this generation should consider how they feel about religion, and how attached they are to their beliefs in general. The Pluto in Sagittarius years were very significant for this group, and it is worth noting how they responded to the changes taking place in society at that time. As with any outer planet in the sign of the archer, the question of belief system is paramount: are they flexible or inflexible, and how will that affect the way they perceive relationship changes?

Uranus in Capricorn   (1988 – 1996)

Uranus and Neptune actually met in Capricorn in 1993, highlighting the changes that Neptune brought to governments and institutions around the world. Looking back on Uranus' years in this sign, we can see that along with Neptune he shared in creating the symbolism of the fall of the Berlin Wall and the Soviet Union, as well as the failed attempts at change in China.

Members of this generation would do well to consider their attitudes towards government and corporations. Strong feelings, whether of support or protest, are likely, although it is also possible that Neptune's influence has helped to create something of an idealized soft focus on these institutions. As with Neptune in this sign, the tensions between career and relationship could be dramatic. As the outer planets get towards the last portion of the zodiac, the emphasis on personal relationships is likely to be less prominent than in the past. Career, and more generally one's role in the world, is likely to take precedence, at least for a time.

Uranus in Aquarius   (1995 – 2003)

Once again, the Internet is the big news with Uranus in Aquarius. The technology boom of the late 1990s is another aspect of this time. Members of this generation are very attuned to technology, and probably have a difficult time getting perspective on the effect of it on their lives. The potentials of technology are great, but there are some pitfalls, too. Among them is the danger that we can live in virtual worlds, living too much of our lives through our computers and not enough through our senses. Whether members of this generation will even see that as a pitfall is an open question. The same questions that Neptune in Aquarius has to deal with apply to this generation, although this group is probably more comfortable with technology as a rule, and will experience a great many of their relationships online.

Keep In Mind...

This brief tour of the astrological generations is meant to get you started thinking about how large cohorts deal may deal with relationship issues, particularly those having to do with the end of partnerships. Some generations, like those with the outer planets were in Libra, may really be focused on this area of life, while other generations may deal with relationship issues—as a generation—more obliquely. It's important to keep in mind that individuals within each astrological generation will have a unique experience and viewpoint on the issue, and a cookie-cutter approach will not work. What we can see is that these generations tend to work with an issue, although they do so from a myriad of individual perspectives.

It is also worth keeping in mind that as a relationship ends, your client may be of one astrological generation, while their partner may be from another. That suggests that they may have very different attitudes towards relationship endings. For example, someone with Uranus and Pluto in Libra may be able to see a wide variety of relationship patterns as valid and be flexible about leaving the partnership, while their partner with the same planets in Virgo could be devoted to one particular image of partnership and have a great deal of trouble separating.

Another consideration is the presence of personal planets in close aspect to the generational planets. Someone with Venus conjunct Uranus and Pluto in Virgo is going to bring the transpersonal, generational energy of the outer planet aspect into their personal life via relationships. Of course, most astrologers would consider the outer planets in aspect to a personal planet, and if we see Venus square to Pluto we might think that control issues are going to be prominent in the person's relationship, or that they may have a tendency towards getting involved with controlling partners, and so on. What I am suggesting, though, is that we remember to read the equation the other way, and recognize the role of the outer planet.

For example, a client with Venus in Cancer may have a rather traditional view of relationship and the feminine, seeing women in the role of mother/wife. If that Venus is square to Pluto in Libra, the tensions around control in relationship may be due to perceptions of what relationship is about. The client may want— or think they want—a very traditional partnership, but they continue to find themselves in relationships with people who have other ideas. With the generational aspect taken into consideration, we may be able to recognize that the client's partner is not necessarily being arbitrarily controlling, but in fact expressing a completely different set of assumptions about relationship.

As I said at the start of this chapter, clients usually want to know about what is happening to them from a very personal perspective, and the generational aspect can be a hard sell. Sometimes, it really is worth insisting that the client reflect on their relationship to their astrological generation, as this speaks so much to their *assumptions* about relationship. Most of the time, we as astrologers will be using this information to gain a better understanding of the dynamics of the relationship ending.

Chapter 13
Approaches to the Astrological Consultation

There are many books about astrological technique, but too few about the astrological consultation process. Astrologers are an individualistic, Uranian lot, and I certainly don't want to tell anyone what to do within their professional practice, but I do think that I can introduce a few ideas about consulting during the break-up process that might be useful.

First, we need to consider if such a consultation would be different from any other session with a client. After all, while it is true that separations are challenging, many of the reasons people consult with astrologers also involve stressful situations. Relationships may speak directly to lunar security needs, but then again so does career. Relationships involve more than one person, but the same is true of virtually all of life, and the difficult coworker, the domineering boss, the ruthless parent, the needy sibling, and a host of other personalities can show up in any session with a client.

As astrologers, we recognize that people have different approaches to the same situation. Someone with much fixed energy around the area of relationship may feel deep trauma while someone with more mutable energy may have an easier time letting go (yet there are exceptions in each case). When it comes down to it, all we know for sure is that this is *potentially* a very difficult time for the client, but it could also be the moment when they get their wings and fly out of a constricting situation. With that in mind, the following are a few considerations that I find worthwhile.

Single Sessions or Astrological Coaching?

The practice of astrology has developed more or less organically. Even our professional associations do not really address the question of how our services should be delivered. Most astrologers seem to have fallen into something like a *medical model*, where the client receives diagnosis and some suggestions for the future within a single session lasting from one to two hours. Follow-up sessions can occur at regular or irregular intervals, for example as the need is sensed by the client or for yearly solar return tune-ups.

This model has much value. It is perhaps the most economically feasible option for many clients, as it involves a one-time charge and perhaps lesser costs for future visits. It also focuses the client and astrologer on the relevant issues, or at least it should focus them. However, there are also limitations to this model. As most astrologers have experienced, a single session can lead to the astrologer pouring out information to the client in a monologue, rather than an interactive dialogue. That makes the consultation into a *reading*, a set of judgments that flow from the astrologer to the client, which is potentially disempowering for the client. Although I have termed this the medical model for astrology, the single-session reading probably owes more to astrology's history in the realm of fortune telling.

Even within a single session, it is certainly possible to open up dialogue and allow the client to express his or her concerns. The astrologer and client thus respond to each other, the client

176

explaining his or her perspective, the astrologer coordinating the client's story with the relevant astrology. Many astrologers are reluctant to ask questions for fear of appearing incompetent, but that is not realistic. When you go to the doctor, or call a plumber, you explain what the problem or concern is in advance. Any professional will try to gather as much relevant information as possible before assessing and treating a condition.

Dialogue also fulfills the basic need to communicate feelings and emotions—and that is one of the reasons clients come to us in the first place. They often seek to confide in a nonjudgmental person, and someone they do not know may serve the purpose better than a friend or relative. Being nonjudgmental seems to be a challenge for many astrologers, although to be fair it is a challenge for most people. Yet it is a key component in providing the other thing clients seek, perspective. We can only offer a unique and helpful perspective to our clients if we can maintain a nonjudgmental and open attitude towards their situation. Without that, we are simply telling them how we feel or what we think is good for them. No doubt, we can bend the meaning of the astrological symbols to support our feelings, but that isn't really of much help to the client. Therefore, opening up dialogue and really listening to the client's concerns is part of the groundwork of a successful consultation.

Given the prevalence of psychological approaches to astrology, it is remarkable that the medical or fortune telling single session model has persisted as long as it has in astrology. Most psychologists see patients over multiple sessions, although the legendary years of time on the analyst's couch have been modified by financial factors as well as the need for faster resolution to conflicts.

We need to be clear that astrologers are *not* psychologists, although some people do practice both professions. For most astrologers, it is important to stay clear of the territory that properly belongs to psychologists and other trained therapists. It is particularly important because both astrologers and psychologists deal with deep emotional issues, and with people who are at important transition points, such as the break-up of a relationship. The basic strategy is to keep in mind that a psychologist works with people who are experiencing *abnormal* psychological states or behavior. Astrologers offer perspective for people who are functioning within a normal range. One helpful rule of thumb from the world of psychology is the "Four Ds" – Deviance, Distress, Dysfunction, and Danger. Although astrologers see people who may be in some state of distress, if there is evidence of significant deviance, dysfunction, or danger, it is time to refer out to the appropriate professional. Even a very high degree of distress should be treated as a warning sign. While I don't encourage many people to enter into the mental health system—for it is not without its problems—knowing some good, open-minded therapists is an important facet of astrological practice.

While psychologists work to bring people back to baseline from a lower level of functioning, astrologers generally work to help bring about *improvements above baseline*. That is, our clients would be fine without us, but they may be better with us. For that reason, I prefer to avoid any reference to psychology altogether and instead use the term *astrological coaching*. Life coaching has become a major trend, so many people are familiar with the term. Yet coaching is also seen in sports, acting, music, and many other fields. Even highly competent experts, like professional baseball players and opera singers, have coaches. These coaches are not addressing pathologies, but are providing additional insights and strategies to help the professionals to excel. I can't think of a better model for astrologers.

Astrological coaching is done over a series of sessions. It is usually helpful to have an initial consultation, where the astrologer works with the entire chart for a comprehensive session that addresses many areas of life and gets a sense of the client (and vice-versa). The coaching sessions themselves are more narrowly focused on a particular goal, such as working through the loss of a relationship. My coaching sessions last an hour, and I ask that clients reserve them in groups of three. I am very flexible about the timing of the sessions, and they may be weekly, monthly, or at irregular intervals, based on the client's needs. During each session, we address the recent developments and strategize for the future, with an emphasis on short-term goals. It is important to relate the goals to the client's astrology, and make sure that they are consistent with both the natal chart and the current transits. Because the time frame of coaching means that I have contact with the client more often than if they were only seeing me yearly or biyearly, it is possible to work with a number of micro-factors, like electional charts for initiating conversations or contacting legal professionals. It is also possible to foresee specific days that may be stressful (say, the moon aspecting natal Saturn) and to develop strategies to deal with the stress. The same goes for opportunities, too, and encouraging clients to make the most of potentially lighter times is just as important as dealing with difficulties.

Break-ups occur over the course of time, and so astrological coaching is an excellent approach. It allows the client to work through the various stages of the loss, from the initial shock, to working with any anger, bargaining, and acceptance (yes, these are Kubler-Ross's stages of grief associated with dying—they are present in many life transitions). On a more basic note, astrological coaching is a good idea because the client needs to both conclude the past relationship and look to the future, and that can be a lot to cover in a single session.

In the end, it is usually the client and not the astrologer that determines the format of the consultation. Whether you do a single session or extended coaching, your role is the same: to offer support and perspective, and to suggest possible avenues for future movement.

One Partner or Both?

Many astrologers only do relationship consultations if both parties are present. They give many reasons for this, including not wanting to give one partner an unfair advantage and not really being able to adequately assess the relationship with input from only one side. I think there is validity to those reasons, but I do see people individually to work with relationship astrology.

Relationship consultations can be very powerful when both partners are present, and I feel it adds a great deal to the dynamic, but it isn't necessary. It is particularly helpful when both partners are enthusiastic about astrology, although if things are going well in the partnership it is okay if one is a bit skeptical. Certainly, you would want to avoid a situation where one partner is skeptical about astrology and the relationship is not in a good place. The astrologer will be met with a wall of doubt, and will probably be accused of siding with the non-skeptical client, something that may in fact be rather hard to avoid doing.

I would note that some astrologers who won't look at the chart of a person who is not present don't mind going into considerable depth about someone seen in the client's chart. That is, the astrologer won't look at your mother's chart if she is not present, but will tell you all about your mother by looking at your moon and fourth house. True, your chart tells you about your mother from *your* perspective, while your mother's actual chart has another level of meaning. But in the long run, any astrological information is still filtered through many levels, including the astrologer and client. Stressing that we are offering perspective rather than fact is important, and makes it easier to see how we can work with the charts of those not present. Additionally, although I *could* envision a situation where the astrologer helps the client leverage the situation against the partner in the short term, I feel that any truly valuable insights are valuable precisely because they create awareness and greater consciousness in the relationship—and that can never be used *against* anyone.

When we talk about a genuine break-up, it is legitimate to assume that there is no longer another partner. There is the client, and there is the *former partner*. In that sense, if a separation has truly occurred, then we will most likely only be able to talk to one of the partners, anyway. If we exclude the available information about the other partner's chart, we are limiting ourselves to half of the story. For example, it would be very useful to know that our client with a Libra ascendant had a partner with both Uranus and Pluto closely conjunct her rising degree.

180

I am sure that some astrologers do some kind of astrological coaching for couples that are in the midst of a break-up, in order to help them get back together. To me, that seems like the kind of goal-directed approach that assumes a judgment about what is best for the client, and it also sounds too much like marriage counseling to me. If you do see both partners in the same session, or sequential sessions, during the break-up, it is important to maintain as much neutrality as possible.

Avoiding Goal-Directed and Judgmental Positions

I've said it before, and I will say it again, because it is one of the most important things we can take into a consultation with us as astrologers: we need to avoid prejudging a situation. We don't know where the greatest opportunity for growth and development lies for the client. They may need to go through a difficult experience in order to come out stronger on the other side. But then again, we don't even know for sure what will be the more difficult experience, as that varies from person to person and from situation to situation. Leave behind assumptions like, *staying together is good, separating is bad.* Our job is to illuminate the situation as much as possible, to throw light wherever we can, and then let the client decide how to make their way through the newly illumined landscape.

These few considerations are intended to get you thinking about the consultation process. There are some things you might want to do, and some things you will want to avoid as you help clients through the process. Creating a real model for astrological consultations is long process we are collectively engaged in as a profession, and my ideas are meant to be short-term and functional.

Chapter 14
Other Partings

Business, Friendship, Family—Other Partings

The ending of personal romantic relationships is the focus of this book, but it makes sense to say a few words about the ending of other types of relationship. Business partnerships, friendships, and family relationships can all result in a quite a bit of stress when they end, especially if there is a clear break-up point rather than simply fading away of the relationship. If the end of these relationships demonstrated processes very distinct from personal relationships we'd need to consider them in separate books, but that isn't the case. One of the premises of this book is that transits of one of the four outer planets will characterize most relationship endings, and that works for all kinds of relationships. What changes are the significators of the partnership, although sometimes they remain the same as in personal relationships.

The following are brief summaries to get you thinking about different kinds of relationship endings. Remember that like personal/romantic relationships we cannot predict the end of a friendship or loss of friends because of outer planet transits, for the transits can actually be very good for friendship. That is especially true of the transits to the relevant houses, which are by conjunction to the house cusp. What we can do is to shed some light on the separation process *if* it happens.

Business Partnerships

Although we may be inclined to think of them very differently in terms of the emotional value we place on them, astrologically business partnerships are viewed very similarly to romantic relationships. In both cases, it is the seventh house and its ruler that signifies the partner, and while commerce may be under the auspices of Mercury and the business itself overseen by Saturn, it is Venus that rules a business partnership.

In fact, it is a little unfair to say that we view business partnerships through a less emotional lens than personal relationships. These can be among the most potent and powerful connections we have with others, particularly to the extent that we invest our time, effort, and identity into the area of career.

We are really considering business *partnerships* in this chapter. That is, this information will be less relevant to people who work for someone else. Career changes can follow somewhat similar patterns, but quitting a job or being fired is different than ending a business partnership. The following also applies most directly to official business partnerships, as when two people form a corporation together. Although there are many other types of partnerships, such as when a supplier partners with a manufacturer or a bank or other source of finances says it is partnering with a company, break-ups really happen amongst individuals. Sometimes, there are more than two people involved in a partnership, and I will leave it to other astrologers to sort out those situations—suffice it to say that it gets complicated but works along more or less the same lines.

In terms of timing, Saturn is often very prominent in the end of business partnerships, which makes sense given the association of the planet with work and business. Significant stresses often occur at the hard aspects of the Saturn cycle, at 7, 14, 22, and 30 years. The latter points in the cycle can coincide with the decision by one partner to retire, something that can cause a great deal of stress if the other partner is not ready to leave the business. Earlier stresses often have to do with the direction the business will take and the division of responsibilities.

When my wife began work as a speech pathologist, she quickly found a job with a dynamic man who led an innovative department in a New York hospital. When he lost his job, they decided to form a private practice together, entering into it as equal partners. For the first seven years (a quarter of the Saturn cycle), the practice was quite successful, although they kept it small and hired only three other therapists to work with them. At that point, however, they decided that the workload on each of them (and the others) was growing too difficult to manage and they expanded, effectively doubling the staff and increasing the range of the practice. Stresses began to emerge as the Saturn opposition approached at 14 years and financial strain was added to ballooning responsibility. As Saturn conjuncted my wife's ascendant, she decided to leave the practice. The break-up was relatively fast in terms of practicality, although it was also less than amicable.

A similar pattern can often be seen in creative partnerships. Lennon and McCartney worked together for a total of about 14 years, from their meeting in 1956 through the break-up of the Beatles in 1970 (The Beatles existed in their canonical John-Paul-George-and-Ringo form for just over 7 years, one quarter of the Saturn cycle). Their break-up was more complex, in part because of Pluto and Uranus aspecting their composite ascendant and midheaven (Paul McCartney's birth time is the subject of some dispute, but he is usually described as having an Aries ascendant). The rancorous break-up of The Beatles was traumatic for a generation that had looked to the group as a model of a future based on peace and love, and in many ways the fate of the band mirrored that of their generation's relationships. From an astrological perspective, we can see that although Saturn may have been the precipitating transit, the ongoing legal battles throughout the 1970s were more consistent with Pluto.

While Saturn is often prominent in the end of business relationships, it pays to see what other outer planets are active at the time in each partner's chart. As with personal relationships, Saturn may precipitate the actual break-up but the other planets may better describe the feelings and lessons of the time. It's important to maintain a focus on the client's needs, as astrologers are often consulted for help with timing important business decisions, and may or may not be interested in the emotional and spiritual implications of their current situation. On the other hand, because there is frequently a strong emotional component to the end of business relationships, it is worth at least exploring some of the implications of Uranus, Neptune, and Pluto.

Of course, the three outermost planets can often have very practical dimensions, too. Neptune may indicate concerns about deception, such as whether the business partner is being fair. One client with a Neptune transit was concerned that her business partner was involved in setting up a new business behind her back. Indeed, it turned out that the woman was building a new business that would eventually compete with my client's venture.

Power plays are perhaps more open, or at least more accepted, in the business world than in personal relationships, and Pluto can often operate more overtly during a break-up, as with the legal wrangles that engulfed Lennon and McCartney. Yet there is also the possibility that Plutonian energy will operate under the surface, as when one partner ventures into dubious legal territory with the business, thereby implicating the other partner.

Uranus is often involved in sudden break-ups, as we would expect. When one partner (or potentially both) has transits to the seventh house or midheaven, they may suddenly decide to leave the business partnership. Unlike personal relationships, where there may or may not be legalities and practicalities involved, the ending of a business relationship will almost always involve a fairly significant amount of paperwork, which can range from merely tedious to protracted legal battles. While that is not fun in any circumstance, it can be particularly irksome to someone in the midst of a Uranus transit—where the desire for freedom is paramount.

Friendships

Friendship doesn't get as much attention as it should in our culture. In astrological consultations, I would estimate that one person in ten asks about friendship. Perhaps we assume that friendships will always be there in one form or another, and most people spend social time with coworkers, neighbors, club members, and others, so that it does indeed seem someone will always be there—and in a sense that is true.

On the other hand, a lasting friendship can be one of life's greatest gifts. I am fortunate to still have some of the same friends I had not only in high school and college, but elementary school. Although we live in different parts of the country and even in different parts of the world, we stay in contact and see each other reasonably often (it's nice having friends in other countries!).

Deep friendships aren't necessarily based on time, however. While there is a degree of comfort and natural affinity for those people with whom we grew up and shared our early life, it is equally possible to have deep connections evolve later in life, and sometimes very fast. Many people find that the people they were close with in childhood head in different directions, or perhaps the problem is that they don't move at all. As adults, we tend to seek out people who share our values and ideals, not just houses on the same block.

Coworker relationships are very interesting. We can spend years at work with the same people, sharing so much on a daily basis, and we may consider them among our closest friends. Yet when one party leaves the work environment, the friendship often dries up very rapidly. Even when people were used to meeting outside of work—for drinks after a long week or for more extended socializing—without the common bond of work there is often little that is shared. This can be a great test of what seemed like a very strong friendship at the time.

While the sixth house may not represent coworkers per se, planets in the house often represent an archetypal coworker that keeps turning up in different employment situations. If the relationship is one of friendship, a transit to that planet could represent a change in the status of the friendship. One client had Saturn in the sixth, and continually found himself confronted with a serious, determined coworker at every job. This person would inevitably take on a role that felt more like a supervisor than a coworker to my client. When my client decided to accept the challenge and really pushed himself forward at one particular job, he surprised himself by becoming friends with his seemingly dour coworker. Another client with Venus in her sixth house would tend to become friends with another female at each job (not unusual except in the weight my client would put on these relationships). When Uranus aspected her Venus, my client's friendship broke up rapidly and in a very Uranian fashion.

An additional consideration with friendships is that they are not usually exclusive. In other words, just because Mary and Peter are friends doesn't mean that either or both of them cannot be friends with Paul. In contrast to (most) romantic/sexual relationships, the assumption of exclusivity is not present in friendships and as a result there is not necessarily the pressure to be in or out of the relationship. When people break off a romantic relationship, at least one of the partners usually moves on to a new partnership at some point, and that closes the door on reviving the original relationship (that isn't always true, of course, but it works to the extent that we think of personal relationships as one-at-a-time, and to the extent that the new partnership is strong and fulfilling). It is generally easier to revive a solid friendship after months or even years, if both people are willing. The major exception to this may be the *Best Friends Forever* kind of friendship, which often does have a vibe of exclusivity to it. Such friendships are sometimes best described by the seventh house and are affected by transits to that house, its ruler, or planets in the house (especially if the planet rules the eleventh).

The key to astrologically understanding friendships, and therefore their endings, is to recognize what house is the most relevant to the relationship. Once we know that, we can look to transits to that house or its ruler for indications about what is going on with the friendship. Friendships can certainly be

187

complex, and at times it may be necessary to look at several factors.

Friendships that go back to childhood or that are based on living in the same neighborhood are third house matters. Look to planets transiting that house or its ruler. It is also worthwhile taking a look at transits to Mercury, which generally signifies peers and one's local cohort, although this will really give more of a general flavor than tell you anything specific about a particular friendship (an exception would be if there was friendship with a distinctly younger person—say for example a younger neighbor).

When people share ideals or have a similar worldview, the friendship is signified by the eleventh house. This is where you would find friends that met at a political meeting, a charity event, working at the local food co-op, and so on. Most enduring friendships for adults fall into this category, regardless of where they got started. For example, two people that meet in college (the ninth house) but remain close friends over the subsequent years have moved into the eleventh house. The point is that there are some shared ideas about things, a natural affinity that keeps the friendship together despite distance in space or time. By contrast, it is possible to get along quite well with the people in one's neighborhood (third house) without really connecting in terms of having a similar worldview. Perhaps you've had the experience of a nice evening turning sour quickly when politics comes up in a conversation—something that is unlikely to happen when the friendship is based in the eleventh house. Of course, people are complex and so are friendships, and it is quite possible that people who get along very well on one axis of thought have difficulties on another. A shared interest in playing music doesn't indicate similar political views, for instance.

Conjunctions by the outer planets to the eleventh house or hard transits to its ruler can indicate difficulty with friendships. Because it is not unusual to have more than one eleventh-house type friendship, it is not unusual for a person to complain of general difficulty with friendship—it is perhaps more likely than concern about one single friend. Still, it is also common for a major rift with one friend to be a kind of signal that there are problems with friendship.

When an outer planet enters the eleventh, there is frequently an extended period of change in this area of life, consistent with planet making the transit. Because the eleventh is not only the house of friendship but also ideals (or worldview), the change in ideals that the outer planet brings often indirectly changes the type of friends with which one seeks to associate. However, it is usually when the planet is entering the house and hanging around the cusp that the most significant changes take place.

Saturn will usually indicate a pairing down of the number of friendships, and those that were hanging on due to sentimentality are often lost. For example, a client with Saturn transiting the eleventh found that a ski trip with his old college roommates, a fun annual adventure for almost ten years, had lost its luster as he realized how much he had changed (and they had not). With Saturn, there is often an acute sense of loneliness and a fear that it will be difficult to make new friends. While a transit of Saturn to the eleventh is indeed unlikely to result in a great number of new friends, it is usually quite possible to develop a couple of deeper connections that will endure for a long time. When Saturn leaves the eleventh, there is often a feeling of relief as friendships become easier (although that sense of relief is balanced by Saturn moving into the twelfth house!).

Uranus in the eleventh often corresponds with an active desire to make changes in one's friendships. Here, there is a desire to expand the scope of friends, and to break out of old routines with the friends one keeps. This is most pronounced when Uranus enters the house, where he will spend about seven years. If there are problems with friendships, the person may be all too ready to dispose of longtime relationships, or may feel slighted by their friends. Although it is possible to repair friendships that go south after the initial shock of Uranus entering the house, the long-term changes to friendship are usually fairly significant. As Uranus leaves the house, it is often possible to look back over the previous seven years and see that one now has a completely different set of friends with a very different set of worldviews.

That is partially true because the eleventh is also the house of goals and ideals, and frequently these also change as Uranus transits the house.

Neptune will transit the eleventh house for about fourteen years, long enough to bring about subtle but profound changes to friendship. The initial experience when Neptune is on the eleventh house cusp may be that friends simply disappear of fade away, without any active or overt separation. People often complain that they don't know what happened, that their friends are not around anymore, or that they have lost touch with them (less likely now with online social networking, but still possible). Unlike Uranus transits, where one group of friends is essentially replaced by another, with Neptune the process can take an extended period of time before new friends are made. Of course, Neptune transits to the eleventh don't necessarily mean losing friends (none of the outer planets transiting the house *necessarily* means losing or changing friends, but this book is about partings), and it can also happen that for a period of time the person is enthralled with a new friend or group of friends, only to have the shine dulled down after a while. It's not that the new friends are not genuine, but often expectations are initially very high.

Pluto transits to the eleventh are of course significant, and it may be that the end of friendships is not at all peaceful. While friends rarely have the kind emotional, practical, and legal commitments to each other that lovers and business partners do, it is entirely possible to have a degree of nastiness between or among friends. Power plays, jealousies, and other Plutonian factors can affect friendships, and these seem to be particularly likely when the two friends are part of a larger group. What Pluto to the eleventh is demanding is that our friendships be real, and that we be real with our friends. If we are being open and genuine, this time can be quite powerful in the development of friendships, but where openness is lacking, trouble can brew. For example, subtle competition among friends can be very problematic when Pluto is in the eleventh house of one friend, or in the composite chart's eleventh house.

When the transit is to the ruler of the eleventh, it is likely that an important friend will have some significant changes taking place in their life. Although a separation between friends is only one of many possible scenarios that the transit can indicate, when it does happen it is usually the case that there is a significant and obvious parting with a specific friend as opposed to a more general change in the overall friendship picture, as is the case with transits through the eleventh house.

Family

Volumes have been written on the astrology of family relationships, and much of what we call *psychological astrology* is devoted to the topic. Any attempt to summarize for the purpose of this book would wind up sounding like a gross oversimplification. The use of planets as general significators for the parents is a somewhat contentious issue, as is the house to use to indicate the mother and father. That siblings are indicated by the third house seems to be more consistently accepted, although one must use derived houses when considering multiple siblings, children, cousins, aunts, and so on. In other words, the sixth house may refer to your oldest aunt, the eighth to her younger sister or brother—whether that would be your maternal or paternal uncle is another question.

What I want to stress is that the same patterns of outer planet transits that characterize personal relationship endings can often be seen when a rift occurs between family members. Because of the complexity of family relationships, I tend to reverse-interpret and use the timing and other information supplied by the client in order to determine the most relevant transit, then use that transit to explain the process. Whatever we see in the chart—and in fact whatever we see in life—is a projection of some aspect of ourselves, and that is especially obvious when it comes to family members. Descriptions of the family member can help to find the relevant significator. Traditional astrology had very specific ideas about who was what in the chart, but models based on traditional family structures (which were always different according to culture) rarely hold true today. Similarly, assumptions about the

191

moon, the sun, Saturn, and other planets are upended by contemporary life. We still have images of security, stability, and so on, and we likely project these onto caregivers, but we can no longer assume that the mother is a stand-in for the lunar function.

This chapter has given you a few hints about how deal with several different types of relationship endings. You can see that the basic patterns are the same as they are for more personal relationships—the main question is what signifies the relationship and the people in it. Ideally, the astrologer will do a comprehensive relationship analysis and come to an understanding of the dynamics of the interaction between the two people. Realistically, however, outside of personal partnerships it is often difficult to get accurate birth information, and the time and effort that goes into doing a relationship analysis may not be warranted without the direct emotional impact of a romantic parting. As I've said, however, friendships, business, and family relationships can carry as much power as a personal partnership, and for some people these are the primary relationships in life.

Epilogue

Love in the Era of Uranus-Pluto

For all practical purposes, we have for millennia all lived virtually our entire lives within the boundaries of Saturn. Motivated by lunar security needs, we have collectively built social structures with the hopes that they will keep us safe. In our personal lives, we have devoted our careers to the purpose of survival: money, prestige, and power all give a semblance of security, however rocky the reality may be. Our relationships, too, have largely been a matter of safety and security, emotional and financial. It is well known that marriage began as an economic transaction, and an honest assessment of it today will show that it very often continues to be about finances as much as about love. Yet even when love is the motivation for a partnership, we frequently see that lunar security needs dominate as we seek emotional—if not financial—security from our partners.

Martial motivation and action, Venusian relating, Jupiterian learning, and even solar energy—the very core or our being—have been devoted to the lunar drive for survival and security, structured by protective, careful, and fearful Saturn. A limiting conservatism that worked to preserve sameness and maintain the status quo colored almost all our activity for a very long time, despite the inevitable change that frustrated the desire for stability.

Yet that is changing, however slowly. When Abraham Maslow described people he called self-actualizers—people who were intent on fulfilling their personal potential and becoming who they truly were—he was talking about a tiny portion of the overall population, almost superheroes compared with their peers. Today, however, I would guess that few people reading (or writing) this book don't have self-actualization as a personal goal, however distant from our actual attitudes and behaviors it is. We are in the process of moving from what Don Beck and Christopher Cowan, in their book *Spiral Dynamics*, call *survival values* to *being values*. While we need to take care of our survival needs, we increasingly focus on being and becoming: our lives and the activities and relationships within them are experienced as meaningful in themselves, not simply subservient to survival. We seek a richness of texture in life that goes beyond preservation of our physical selves. We want to become more (and better) than we are at present.

When being values begin to predominate, we are no longer content to simply survive, and we are not happy with the short hours left at the end of the day, or at the end of our work life, to pursue that which is deeply fulfilling. Even our pleasures are likely to leave us flat after a while, to the extent that they arise from survival needs: and after all, food, sex, and many other pleasurable activities all stem from personal or species level survival. We begin to move away from simple satisfaction of needs, and towards a more refined and meaningful experience. Thus, when food is the issue, we may on the one hand seek to have healthy food that is lower in fat, salt, and sugar than more immediately satisfying junk food, while on the other hand we move towards the subtle experiences of quality foods. With sex, the need to fulfill the biological urge to mate for reproduction of the species is transmuted in more subtle realms of pleasure that

194

address a range of physical, emotional, and spiritual facets of being (a comparison of how long the act of sex lasted as recently as the steamy works of D.H. Lawrence in the early 20th century with today's expectations is very instructive).

This change from the security-oriented focus on survival to the focus on being is truly a new part of the human experience. In the past, those who wanted to self-actualize had to do so within tightly prescribed limits. It is true that religious orders would accept as monks and nuns those who wanted to devote themselves to a kind of self-actualization. The monastery would take care of survival needs, but it would also define the ultimate goal. You couldn't show up at a Zen monastery and declare that you felt the need to be a painter or musician, and you couldn't walk into a Catholic monastery with the intention of exploring your sexuality.

In our relationships perhaps more than in any other area of life, we have difficulty moving from survival to being needs. Part of us holds on to the need for security, for the partner to always be there: the partner as the parent we had or the parent we didn't have. Yet we are also becoming more aware that our needs and wants as individuals are evolving, and our partners may either fail to evolve or may move in different directions from us. As our relationship lives extend from the mid-teens forward, we can look to seven or more decades of relating. Can we expect that the same person who bedazzled us in high school or college will be the partner for us as we enter midlife or as we round the corner of our seventh decade? It is lovely to think that we may grow old sharing our lives—*wrinkling together*, as one client put it—with the same person in an ongoing emotional solidarity, but how realistic is it?

However, it is also true that we recognize that moving frequently from one relationship to another is not without its problems. While we may find it easier to meet our present needs with such an approach, it is also apparent that without some continuity our partnerships may lack depth. It can be tricky to separate legitimate needs for personal growth from more momentary desires for novelty. Avoiding stability and consistency can be just as problematic as demanding them.

In the minds of astrologers, the Uranus-Pluto square that dominates the second decade of the 21st century is most closely associated with significant political, economic, and social changes, and those are indeed the areas that are most obviously in a process of transformation at this time. We should remember, however, that relationships, and particularly marriage, are also social structures (you remember the old joke about marriage being an institution), and so are part of the landscape of deep changes. The growing acceptance of gay marriage both socially and legally is but one example of the transformation of relationship.

The breakdown and rebuilding of social structures is something that many of us look forward to on one level or another, but most of us also have our limits. It may be easy to see problems with the extremes of growth-oriented capitalism and the unchecked power of large corporations—it is more difficult to wish the downfall of the system when one's retirement account is closely tied to the success of those very corporations. When it comes to relationships, we are facing deep transformation in an area of life where many of us are least comfortable with change. Significantly, both Uranus and Pluto are beyond the boundaries of Saturn, and one of the most unsettling thing about the square between these outer planets is that no matter what direction we move towards, going back to the status quo is not an option.

As we move forward into this unknown and unknowable territory, we would do well to have some compassion for ourselves and for others. Yes, most people have unresolved security needs around the area of relationship, and certainly we continue to cleave to the ideal of a single life partner that will fulfill all of our needs. If some of those needs are not met, many of us are willing to forego them in order to maintain emotional continuity. But increasingly we recognize the importance of personal growth and the evolution of our soul, the need to actualize our potentials. Within that context, we begin to realize that relationships can hold us back as well as help us to move forward. We seek to relate with those people who can act as our teachers, our students, and our companions on this amazing, frightening, beautiful journey.

CPSIA information can be obtained
at www.ICGtesting.com
Printed in the USA
LVHW092138050122
707976LV00019B/155